Mathias of Maryland

D1457996

Mathias of Maryland

Remembering a Lincoln Republican in the Senate

Edited by FREDERIC B. HILL *and*
MONICA HEALY

Foreword by Norman J. Ornstein

McFarland & Company, Inc., Publishers
Jefferson, North Carolina

Library of Congress Cataloging-in-Publication Data

Names: Hill, Frederic B., editor. | Healy, Monica, 1949– editor.
Title: Mathias of Maryland : remembering a Lincoln Republican in the Senate / edited by Frederic B. Hill and Monica Healy.
Other titles: Remembering a Lincoln Republican in the Senate
Description: Jefferson, North Carolina : McFarland & Company, Inc., Publishers, 2024 | Collection of essays by Michael R. Klipper and 14 others. | Includes bibliographical references and index.
Identifiers: LCCN 2024002645 | ISBN 9781476694207 (print) ∞ ISBN 9781476651989 (ebook)
Subjects: : Mathias, Charles McCurdy, Jr., 1922–2010. | Legislators—United States—Biography. | United States. Congress. Senate—Biography. | United States—Politics and government—1945–1989. | Maryland—Biography. | BISAC: HISTORY / United States / Civil War Period (1850-1877) | BIOGRAPHY & AUTOBIOGRAPHY / Political
Classification: LCC E840.8.M37 M37 2024 | DDC 328.73/092—dc23/eng/20240212
LC record available at https://lccn.loc.gov/2024002645

British Library cataloguing data are available

ISBN (print) 978-1-4766-9420-7
ISBN (ebook) 978-1-4766-5198-9

Front cover: Senator Charles Mathias (R–Maryland), February 1, 1969 (Bettman Archives)

Printed in the United States of America

McFarland & Company, Inc., Publishers
  Box 611, Jefferson, North Carolina 28640
    www.mcfarlandpub.com

**Charles McCurdy Mathias, Jr.,
U.S. Senator (R–MD),
1969–1987.**

"As our case is new, so we must think anew. We must disenthrall ourselves, and then we shall save our country."

—*Abraham Lincoln, December 1862,*
Message to Congress upon eve of passage
of the Emancipation Proclamation

"There have been actions over the past few years that have caused some in positions of power and responsibility to forget that the highest loyalty of an American public servant is not to any personality whether he be a President or a general or a senator; nor is it to any organization, department, agency or party. His first loyalty is to the law of the land built upon constitutional foundations by Thomas Jefferson, George Washington, Alexander Hamilton, George Mason and other great men of our revolutionary past."

—*Senator Charles McC. Mathias, Jr.,*
during Watergate crisis, 1973–74

Table of Contents

Acknowledgments

We are deeply indebted to the enthusiastic participation of all of the contributors to this composite biography of one of the 20th century's most outstanding and independent senators.

With passage of a significant period of time, all of these members and former members of Congress, former staff members and journalists happily consented to reach back and explore the remarkable career, character and convictions of the man known to all as "Mac" Mathias. The result, we are convinced, is a fitting tribute to that career and his achievements—not only long overdue but all the more timely in the context of today's broken and harshly divided political situation in the United States.

We could not have succeeded in this quest to bring honor and recognition to an outstanding senator without the support, patience and editing assistance from our spouses, George Hager and Marguerite (Marty) Hill. George, a long-time journalist and author, carefully reviewed and helped edit many of the essays, enhancing the quality of the work. Marty provided consistent advice, editorial review and technical support throughout work on the book.

We also greatly appreciate the help of the senator's two sons, Charles and Rob, who were readily available whenever we reached out to them and provided wise counsel. They were very helpful in numerous ways, including being a great resource in providing information about their father's personal history (including pictures), his family and his ancestors, material that would otherwise have been impossible to find.

This project could not have been accomplished without the rigor and support of Paul McCardell, the head (and only) librarian now at *The Baltimore Sun*. Promptly and precisely, Paul supplied us—and many of our contributors—with hundreds of articles on Senator Mathias' near three-decade-long career. We also relied heavily on the *Washington Post*'s extensive coverage of Mathias' career. The *Chesapeake Quarterly* was an invaluable resource.

We deeply appreciate the assistance and encouragement of very busy and hard-working senior staff assistants to current and former members of Congress, including Trish Russell, chief of staff to Senator Chris Van Hollen (D–MD); Alexis Covey-Brandt and Adam Weissmann with Representative Steny Hoyer (D–MD); Melissa Baranowski, executive assistant to Senator Barbara Mikulski (D–MD); and Ann Pendley, executive assistant to Senator Alan Simpson (R–WY).

We benefited from terrific assistance and advice from a number of journalists and governmental leaders who led us to important contacts, sources and facts. They include Tom Horton, a nationally respected writer on environmental matters and former *Baltimore Sun* reporter; Andrew Yarrow, a leading author and former *New York Times* reporter; Kathleen Kennedy Townsend, former Maryland lieutenant governor; Steve Luxenberg, author and *Washington Post* editor; Ambassador Frederic Hof, former senior official in the State and Defense departments and now professor at Bard College; and Ambassador Roman Popadiuk, the first envoy to Ukraine, executive director of the George H.W. Bush Presidential Library Foundation and today president of the Diplomacy Center Foundation, which oversees the National Museum of American Diplomacy.

Jan Scruggs' and Robert Doubek's books on the struggle to create the Vietnam Veterans Memorial provided helpful background material.

This volume could not have been completed without the support and research of James Stimpert, Senior Reference Archivist at Special Collections, Johns Hopkins University's Sheridan Libraries, and the technical and editing assistance of Lauren Leatham, Cornell University class of 2023.

Also, we want to thank a number of friends and colleagues who offered advice and assistance at various points: Tom and Ash Karhl, Bath (Maine) Printing; Chris Ponticas; Elaine Weiss; Thomas Edsall; Steven Weissman; and Stephens Broening. Others who assisted include James C. Clark, Jeff Price, Randy Dove, Paul Carliner, Ken Mannella, Joe Peraino, Kevin Kelly, Sherry Kaiman, John Moag, Garth Neuffer, Mark Wasserman and Charlie Stek.

We are thankful for the sound counsel of Arnold "Skip" Isaacs, a veteran *Baltimore Sun* correspondent and author, who first suggested McFarland to us, and also for the exemplary professional care and oversight of the book by Gary Mitchem, Senior Editor, Lisa Camp, Executive Editor, Whitney Wallace and their team at McFarland.

We benefited from the comprehensive collection of comments, remarks and quotations of Senator Mathias that was organized by two former staff members, Peggy Nalle and Alan Dessoff.

Any errors in this text are wholly by oversight and the responsibility of the authors.

Foreword

Norman J. Ornstein

I came to Washington and the Senate in the fall of 1969, just months after Mac Mathias became a senator from Maryland. It was a tumultuous time, with Vietnam convulsing and dividing the nation and creating deep divisions between Republican president Richard M. Nixon and a Congress with Democrats in the majority of both houses. But the divisions on the war were not partisan. Among the strongest supporters of Nixon's policies in Vietnam were Southern Democrats, including powerhouses like John Stennis, James Eastland, Richard Russell and Herman Talmadge. And the ardent opponents included liberal and moderate Republicans like Mark Hatfield, Jacob Javits, Charles Goodell—and Mac Mathias.

The parties I saw and dealt with that year in Congress were, as the cliché goes, broad tents. The Democrats had nearly as many conservatives, mostly Southerners, called "Boll Weevils" for the insect that plagues cotton, as well as liberals from other regions. Of the 43 Republicans in the Senate, a dozen or so were liberal or moderate stalwarts, including, along with those above, Ed Brooke, Margaret Chase Smith, Clifford Case, Howard Baker, John Sherman Cooper and George Aiken.

In 1970, I worked as a congressional fellow for George McGovern, dividing my time between party reform and efforts to end American involvement in Vietnam. Our work on an amendment to end the war, done out of the Methodist Building, a stone's throw from the Senate office buildings and the Capitol, meant that we regularly met with those liberal and moderate senators as we worked to build public and Senate support over the bitter objections of Nixon and his acolytes. It was my first real acquaintance with the men (and one woman) of deep conviction and moral courage willing to take on their own president, and a lot of their own party faithful and constituents, over a matter of principle.

Of course, this issue cutting across party lines did not mean Congress, or the broader political system, was nonpartisan; partisanship was

1

still a core feature of politics, and the partisan divide was growing deeper. Government had become bitterly divided, and outside forces had begun using negative campaigns to exploit wedge issues and inflame party bases. In 1970, for example, appealing for "law and order," with its racial innuendo, was particularly effective.

But despite the negative messages—mild in comparison to today's campaigns—and the acrimony that led three or so years later to the beginning of an impeachment inquiry against Nixon, there were still bright spots of bipartisan agreement. These included historic environmental laws such as the Clean Air Act, the Clean Water Act, and the Marine Mammal Act, as well as the creation of the Environmental Protection Agency, Title IX rights for women, and revenue sharing. The bitter acrimony over Vietnam between freshman Republican Senator Bob Dole and Democrat George McGovern that I witnessed first-hand in 1970 was replaced not long thereafter by a partnership and friendship that lasted until McGovern's death in 2012. The link that was strong enough to overcome their differences was their shared desire to end hunger in America, especially via food stamps.

When Watergate emerged in 1973, the Senate managed an exemplary bipartisan inquiry, with Democrat Sam Ervin working hand in glove with Republican Howard Baker, and a staff where the majority's Sam Dash was able to work as well with his counterpart Fred Thompson. Despite the strong desire of Senate Republicans to protect their president, Baker and Republican leader (and moderate) Hugh Scott made sure the investigation was fair and thorough—and, of course, it was devastating to Nixon.

During the decades that followed, I wrote extensively about Congress and specifically about the Senate, and I came back from academia to work there, as a staffer and then staff director on the select committee established in 1976 to study and reform the Senate's committee system—one with 12 members, evenly divided between Democrats and Republicans. In that endeavor, while working directly for the committee chair Adlai Stevenson III and member Gaylord Nelson, I also worked very closely with Republicans Bill Brock, Bob Packwood and Pete Domenici. Our disagreements were never partisan, and these senators were distinguished by their belief in the importance and integrity of the Senate—a norm political scientist Donald R. Matthews called "institutional patriotism" in his seminal 1960 book *U.S. Senators and Their World*.

As I worked in the Senate, I came to know Mac Mathias, including his efforts on the Rules Committee to make the Senate work better, even as I watched him interact with his colleagues and develop his reputation as one of the most thoughtful, honest, decent and diligent people in the body. As the essays in this book make clear, Mathias had his capable hands on some of the most significant policy advances of the post-war era, and he was also instrumental in efforts such as the creation of the Vietnam Veterans Memorial. Mathias' lodestar was his conscience, and no amount of political pressure would shake him when it came to values such as civil rights, voting rights, and protecting the Chesapeake Bay and the broader environment. He also led or was a key soldier in fights to oppose unjust and unwise wars, support democracy and human rights abroad and uphold ethical standards. Following those principles, he frequently drove Republican presidents to distraction, including Ronald Reagan, with whom he clashed over, among other things, so-called "tough on crime" legislation and international human rights.

I sometimes reflect on the senators I knew who worked alongside Mac. Giants like Phil Hart, Jake Javits, Ted Kennedy, Ed Muskie, Howard Baker, Bob Dole, Hugh Scott, Mike Mansfield, Mark Hatfield, Margaret Chase Smith, Alan Simpson, Hubert Humphrey, Walter Mondale, John Glenn, Dick Lugar, Sam Nunn, Pat Moynihan, William Cohen, Jack Danforth, and Nancy Kassebaum, who were role models of public service—as many Republicans as Democrats. I prized my relationships with many of them and worked on many reform and other public policy issues with them, as I did with Mathias. Most were loyal partisans, but their desire to work together to solve pressing problems and to maintain integrity and ethical standards in the Senate—that "institutional patriotism"—was clear and obvious.

The contrast between the Mathias era and the Senate of today is stark. The parties, of course, are very different. There are no conservative Democrat "Boll Weevils"—no John Stennises, Richard Russells, Jim Eastlands, etc. The closest is Joe Manchin, but he is just one of 50 senators, not 40 percent or more of the Democratic Caucus. On the Republican side, there is no Mathias, Javits, Hatfield or Brooke, much less a Baker or a Scott. The closest thing to a moderate is Maine's Susan Collins, but she is far from moderate in her overall voting record or rhetoric. In other words, Collins is no Mathias. Nor are any of her colleagues. Over the decades, the Senate has become polarized, as the parties have sorted into more extreme ideological cohorts.

But polarization alone does not mean gridlock, the absence of problem-solving, disdain for the norms and traditions of the Senate, or putting party over country. For example, two senators Mathias served with—Ted Kennedy and Orrin Hatch—managed, despite their stark differences in party and ideology, to work together to create the landmark

Children's Health Insurance Program, or CHIP, by recognizing the problem, finding some common ground, and horse-trading to come up with a balanced bill.

Over the past few years, the Republicans in the Senate who have the intelligence, background and depth to compare to their admired predecessors have included legislators such as Lamar Alexander, Rob Portman, Roy Blunt and Mitt Romney. But other than Romney, the others regularly voted in concert with Donald Trump's desires and interests, acting more like apparatchiks than independent-minded, problem-solving senators, saying little or nothing about Trump's corruption and links to the world's most vicious autocrats and dictators. And even Romney, whose candor about Trump has been refreshing, voted for a slew of ethically challenged and unqualified Trump nominees for the executive branch and the courts. Politics in the Senate, as in the country, have become tribalized, where the other side is seen as evil, not just people with a different viewpoint. The Republican Party, in particular, has become a kind of cult, where the fear of being shunned or excommunicated keeps members in line, losing their ethical compasses.

To be sure, there are times when the Senate finds broad bipartisan compromise, as it did in 2021 with the infrastructure bill. But those examples are few compared with the Mathias era. Confirmation of executive and judicial nominees has become dominated by obstruction and division, and important efforts such as raising the debt limit have moved from sure things to weapons for hostage-taking and partisan leverage, endangering the full faith and credit of the United States. The Senate that systematically uncovered the outrages of Richard Nixon—where the Senate, after the House Judiciary Committee hearings, sent Hugh Scott and Barry Goldwater to the White House to convince Nixon to resign—is far from the Senate that saw Republicans rally around Donald Trump through two impeachment hearings, including many senators who publicly admitted Trump's miscreance. There is no Howard Baker, Hugh Scott or Barry Goldwater in today's Republican Senate Conference.

Because of his decency, integrity and intellect, Mac Mathias had no trouble winning election after election as a Republican in a state that became increasingly blue. He was not alone in Maryland; another example for decades was Mathias' congressional district when he lived in Chevy Chase. After Mathias, the liberal-leaning Montgomery County was also represented by moderate Republicans Gilbert Gude, Newton Steers and Connie Morella, until Morella was defeated by Democrat Chris Van Hollen, who now occupies Mathias' seat in the Senate. And Maryland still can elect Republicans statewide, as it showed when Republican Larry Hogan,

Jr., became governor. Hogan's father, Larry Hogan, Sr., also a Republican, served as a congressman from the 5th district, including Prince George's County, and distinguished himself by voting for all three articles of impeachment against Richard Nixon in the House Judiciary Committee.

But the country as a whole, and the Senate in particular, would not easily accommodate a Charles McC. Mathias today. A liberal Republican, putting country over party, voting his conscience even when it clashed with the narrow interests of a president of his party, is simply nowhere to be found in either the Senate or the House. But one thing is clear to anyone who knew and worked with Mac Mathias: He would not bend his values or his behavior one iota to fit the demands of his tribe if he were here and in the Senate today.

Norman J. Ornstein is an emeritus scholar at the American Enterprise Institute. A political scientist, he has worked in Congress and has been writing about American politics for more than 50 years. Ornstein was elected as a fellow of the American Academy of Arts and Sciences in 2004. He was named one of the top 100 global thinkers in 2012 by Foreign Policy *Magazine. His many books include the* New York Times *bestsellers* It's Even Worse Than It Looks *(with Thomas Mann) and* One Nation After Trump: A Guide for the Perplexed, the Disillusioned, the Desperate and the Not-Yet-Deported *(with Mann and E.J. Dionne).*

Preface

FREDERIC B. HILL *and* MONICA HEALY

We embarked on this project because we believe that Senator Mathias, whom both of us worked for, stood out among his peers as a courageous, ethical, principled senator, often bucking the leadership of his own party, putting country and Constitution over party, a rare quality today.

The book is a collection of essays by current and former members of Congress, senior staff members and a journalist—all of whom worked with the senator or reported on his activities. Including a foreword by a leading scholar on American politics, the book captures Mathias' character and career but also offers a first-hand look at his engagement in key issues of the 1960s, '70s and '80s.

Mathias took a leadership role in civil rights, voting rights, and human rights both here and abroad. He pushed funding and policy changes to create robust anti-poverty and social programs. A strong advocate for environmental programs, he is considered by many the father of the Chesapeake Bay program. Mathias was an outspoken critic of the Vietnam War, led the congressional effort to establish the Vietnam Veterans Memorial, and was one of the first Republicans to speak out about Watergate. He was a lone voice in voting against a sweeping Republican-led crime bill. He supported bipartisan policies in national security, especially in Middle East peace efforts and nuclear arms control. Due to his independent attitude and bipartisan spirit, he easily won all of his elections to the House and Senate in a heavily Democratic state.

The book concludes with the eulogy by Vice President Joseph Biden at the memorial service for Senator Mathias on February 2, 2010. Biden's moving, heartfelt remarks reflect his and so many senators'—Republican and Democratic—deep respect for Mathias and his reverence for the Constitution, the rule of law and bipartisan spirit.

This is the story of one member of Congress, but he wasn't unusual back then. He was part of an influential group of moderate and liberal

Republicans in the House and Senate who regularly worked across the aisle to get things done.

That Republican Party does not exist today. In fact, today's party is a shell of what it once was. It has been on a downward spiral since Ronald Reagan shifted the party to the right and House Speaker Newt Gingrich led it to a new level of tribalism and division to what we have today with the dangerous, far-right politics of Donald Trump.

The 2022 midterm elections gave us some hope that voters are turning their backs on extremist candidates and will support moderate candidates who respect bipartisanship and civility. Our goal with this book is to remind readers about what the Republican Party once was and could be again.

Biographic Profile

FREDERIC B. HILL *and* MONICA HEALY

Let a renowned journalist capture the essence of Mac Mathias, one of the giants of the Senate in the 1970s and 1980s and perhaps the most accomplished member of Congress in the state of Maryland's history.

In a 1985 column titled "The Republican Outsider," *The Washington Post*'s Meg Greenfield recalled a memorable trip she took with Senator Mathias to a Civil War battlefield that evokes his quick mind, even-keeled character and deep-seated, almost professorial devotion to the Constitution and American history.

On a "truly freezing December afternoon" in 1970, the then–first-term senator escorted Greenfield on a tour of the Antietam National Battlefield Park after a drive in "the wreck of a car he drove with holes in the floorboards from the goats he frequently transported" around his farm. The senator was strongly opposed to a *Post* editorial that disagreed with his call for doubling the size of the battlefield to include the site of Clara Barton's field hospital during the Civil War. "What I remember best is the loving preoccupation of Mathias with every detail of the early American farmhouse, its construction and furnishings, and his utter familiarity and enthusiasm for the countryside we traversed. I almost forgave him the certainty of pneumonia."

Closing her column, she puzzled over the reasons why the Republican Party eventually came to sideline Mathias from key positions just because he consistently stood up for the rule of law, the Bill of Rights and campaign finance reform and became one of the first members of the GOP to back the Watergate investigation.

She remained unable to put her finger on the reason—noting that his independence and bipartisan spirit were not all that different from other Republican leaders in the Senate such as Richard Lugar, Alan Simpson, Nancy Kassebaum and William Cohen. "The Republicans, riding high in Washington [at the time], should ask themselves how it was that so many of them found this man's American political fundamentalism so frightening."

* * *

Charles McCurdy Mathias, Jr., naval officer, lawyer, congressman, senator, and statesman, died on January 25, 2010, after an extended battle with Parkinson's disease. He was 87.

Truly a man for all seasons, Senator Mathias served in Congress for 26 years, four terms in the House as a representative from Frederick, his native part of Maryland, and three terms as U.S. senator.

He decided to retire in 1986 due in part to the increasingly right-ward shift of his party. But he was also frustrated with the need to raise ever increasing amounts of campaign money. "Mac" Mathias was widely known for his erudition, integrity, broad-gauged knowledge of critical domestic and foreign policy challenges and a principled, independent character that gained him the respect of political leaders of all persuasions.

He early on supported controversial civil rights legislation and opposed the Vietnam War, both uncommon positions for a Republican. He supported peace in the Middle East and sanctions against the White minority regime in South Africa. Mathias served Maryland and the nation for nearly three decades with unbending attention to human need. Throughout his career he embodied deep respect for the Constitution and the rule of law, courage—and that most enduring of traits—a sense of humor.

After a rigorous fight to reform campaign finance in 1974, an election in which Mathias refused to accept contributions in excess of $100, Mike Mansfield, the leader of the Democratic Party in Congress, said the senator from Maryland "has become the conscience of the Senate."

Largely due to his firm bipartisanship, Mathias won that 1974 election with 57 percent of the vote in a heavily Democratic state. Safely popular, Mathias went on to lead the Maryland delegation throughout his career and tackle a long list of challenging issues in both domestic and foreign policy.

There have been very few Republican senators of such stature, independence and dedication to the national interest since the senator's retirement in 1986.

* * *

"Mac" Mathias, as he came to be known, was born on July 24, 1922, one of three children of Frederick, Maryland, lawyer Charles Mathias, Sr., who was active in the Republican Party. His mother, Theresa McElfresh Trail Mathias, was a discriminating collector of early American furniture.

His political pedigree had deep roots. An ancestor served in Washington's Continental Army. His great-grandfather, Colonel Charles E. Trail, ran

Left: Charles E. Trail, Mathias' great-grandfather and a Republican leader in Maryland in the Lincoln era (Mathias Family). *Right:* William Fiske Bradford, Governor of Massachusetts, 1947–1949, and father of Ann Bradford Mathias (Wikimedia).

for the Maryland senate in 1864 on the anti-slavery Republican Party ticket headed by Abraham Lincoln. His grandfather was one of the leaders of Maryland's Republican Party, and Senator Mathias' wife, Ann Hickling Bradford, whom he married in 1958, was the daughter of a governor of Massachusetts, Robert Fiske Bradford (1947–49), a descendant of the second governor of the Plymouth Colony, William Bradford, who was governor of the colony off and on from 1621 to 1657.

Senator Mathias enlisted in the U.S. Coast Guard in December 1942 (a year to the day after Pearl Harbor). He was assigned

Mathias as a U.S. Coast Guard enlistee, 1942 (Mathias Family).

Mathias as a U.S. Navy reserve officer, with wife Ann and son Charles, 1962 (Mathias Family).

to a V-12 unit at Yale University and then transferred to the U.S. Navy. He attended officer candidate school at Columbia University and was commissioned as an ensign in the Navy there. He served in the Philippines and Japan during the occupation.

His strong, lifelong support for nuclear arms control is partly explained by his personal experience when a ship he was on visited Hiroshima in late October 1945, following the dropping of the atomic bomb.

He and eight other officers on the USS *Appalachian* toured the ruins at Hiroshima after the amphibious force flagship landed occupation troops, and he described his visit in a letter to his parents that was reprinted in *The Frederick News-Post*.

"Hiroshima has to be seen to be believed," he wrote. "The thought that what was done there was done by a single bomb is frightening, and awesome. Hiroshima looks like some malevolent giant had pounded it all to dust with an enormous mallet. The only recognizable objects in the ruins are some human bones, some roof tiles and some bits of household china that seem to have been immune to the general destruction."

He concluded his naval career as an officer on the battleship USS *New Jersey* in post-war Europe.

* * *

Senator Mathias earned his bachelor's degree from Haverford College. He received a law degree from the University of Maryland in 1949. He served as a city attorney in Frederick and an assistant attorney general of Maryland during the 1950s before running successfully for the state House of Delegates in 1958.

Mathias made an early impression for his devotion to principle and American history when, as a young delegate in the Maryland House, he delivered a homily to Abraham Lincoln on the late president's 150th birthday (February 12, 1959). "This may be the lesson of Lincoln—that each of

Ann holding Robert, Mathias holding Charles, 1962 (Mathias Family).

The senator and his sons Charles (directly in front of his father) and Robert on the C & O Canal (Mathias Family).

us must live by and for our principles, however they may be shaped by our individual philosophies. Not every one of us can be born a prodigy, but every man and woman in this chamber can live a life true to his or her convictions."

Citing repeated GOP failures in Maryland and noting that Mathias was one of only seven Republican delegates in the General Assembly, William Prendergast, a national Republican leader, made a comment in 1959 that foreshadowed 21st-century party troubles: "The Republican Party in Maryland is sick unto death. There is a glimmer of hope in a promising young Frederick County delegate [Mathias]."

Early Years in Congress

Mathias was elected to Congress in 1960, representing a district that included both conservative western Maryland and liberal Montgomery County. In his last House term, redistricting made his district mostly western Maryland.

He arrived in Washington the same year that John F. Kennedy narrowly defeated Richard M. Nixon for the presidency. Mathias was sworn in on January 3, 1961, accompanied by his wife Ann and his parents, becoming the first member of Congress from Frederick County since 1883.

Early in his first term, the new congressman gave an interview that reflected a keen intellect but a folksy manner that served him well throughout a career in which he would win eight straight elections in a heavily Democratic state.

Noting the long congressional days, especially with a regular commute from his dairy farm near Frederick, he said, "As a farmer, I'm an early riser. I'm up with the chickens, but I don't go to bed with the hens."

Candidate Mathias and Ann, campaigning in Frederick with President Eisenhower for Mathias' first term in the House, 1960 (Mathias Family).

Mathias (third from left) with President John F. Kennedy and others, 1962 (Mathias Family).

It did not take the young Republican long to make a name for himself. Keenly aware of the ravages of segregation in his own state, Mathias pushed early on for strong bipartisan support for civil rights legislation. He was a key player in enactment of the two landmark laws of the civil rights movement: the Civil Rights Act of 1964 and the Voting Rights Act of 1965.

Mathias and his liberal Republican colleague on the House Judiciary Committee, John Lindsay of New York, were vocal in their criticism of the Kennedy administration's overly cautious approach on civil rights legislation. Mathias and Lindsay pushed the Kennedy administration to introduce the bill that became the 1964 Civil Rights Act. Mathias then worked assiduously with one of his mentors, William McCulloch (R–OH), the ranking member of the House Judiciary Committee, and with Lindsay and other Republicans to secure its enactment.

Mathias was similarly aggressive and successful on the voting rights front. He was one of 15 members who visited Selma, Alabama, in February 1965 to support the Rev. Martin Luther King's drive to register Black voters. Upon his return from Selma, Mathias proposed a bill to give the federal government the power to send voting registrars into districts where

Blacks were being routinely deprived of the right to vote. Shortly thereafter, the Johnson administration sent a comprehensive voting rights bill to the Hill that was signed into law in August 1965.

While Senate leaders such as Mike Mansfield of Montana, a Democrat, and Everett Dirksen of Illinois, the Republican leader, drew major credit for the bill's stunning bipartisan support, Mathias was one of the youngest members of either chamber to be cited as a critical factor in passage of the legislation.

Of course, this was a different Republican Party than the one that exists now. Several civil rights bills had been passed during the Eisenhower administration, largely due to the backing of many liberal and moderate Republicans who voted with Northern and Western Democrats to sideline the segregationist bloc of Southern Democrats.

Mathias was a leader in the 1970 and 1975 extensions of the 1965 voting rights law. He was therefore the logical choice to serve as the Senate's lead sponsor of the bill to again renew and amend the 1965 Act. Mathias—with his long-term ally on social justice and civil rights Ted Kennedy (D–MA)—introduced the bill and the Senate approved it on June 18, 1982, by a 95–8 vote. President Reagan signed it into law shortly thereafter.

Mathias continued to be active in civil rights throughout his career. Reflecting on his life in the Senate in a 1987 *Baltimore Sun* interview, he said, "I would think that my involvement in the civil rights movement in the '60s may have had a more profound impact on American life than almost anything else I touched during this 26-year period. By the time I left Congress we hadn't achieved full racial justice or equality, but we had at least torn down the racial barriers."

The Vietnam War and the 1968 Campaign

Mathias was one of about a dozen moderate to liberal Republican House members to oppose the Johnson administration's escalation of the war against North Vietnam. The group went from mild criticism of the administration's early prosecution of the war to increasingly stronger opposition to various decisions, coming out strongly for a staged end to the bombing of the North in 1967.

While Mathias had voted for the 1964 Gulf of Tonkin resolution, which gave Johnson effective authority to conduct the war, he became increasingly skeptical of the administration's strategy and eventually emerged as a leading opponent.

He regularly argued for an end to the war and the use of the billions of dollars instead to "build a more prosperous and progressive society" at home. It would be much better, he said, "to build better homes in Baltimore, expand jobs and clean up the Chesapeake Bay."

The Vietnam War was a major focus of Mathias' decision in 1968 to challenge Democratic senator Daniel Brewster—an old friend in whose wedding he had served as best man. Although a better-known Republican was considered more likely to oppose Brewster, Mathias became the GOP candidate after winning the primary handily.

Mathias didn't let friendship and personality get in the way of the major issues he addressed during a tough campaign. From the start, he blasted Brewster's support for the Johnson war strategy, calling him "a mouthpiece for the administration." Bruised by Mathias' clear and sustained call for a de-escalation, Brewster shifted his position away from full support for the war.

Mathias won the editorial backing of *The Baltimore Sun* in large part due to his forceful anti-war stance. Mathias, the influential paper said, "is a legislator of independent thought, imagination and resourcefulness whose reputation on Capitol Hill is already high."

Despite endorsements for Brewster from organized labor and most Maryland political organizations, Mathias won by nearly 100,000 votes over his Democratic rival and an independent candidate in the heavily Democratic state.

* * *

Senator Mathias played a major role—especially for a first-term senator—in important debates and initiatives during the Vietnam War, which ended in 1975 after the embarrassing withdrawal of U.S. forces and the ultimate collapse of the corrupt South Vietnamese government.

In his very first term in the Senate, in 1969, he won recognition from senior members of both parties for his quiet, resolute pursuit of a common-sense policy on the war and a president's authority to conduct it.

Democratic majority leader Mike Mansfield quickly threw his support behind a Mathias resolution in 1969 to repeal a host of congressional acts that granted near-total authority to a president to use military force. Mathias had called for restoration of Congress' role in war decisions and for doing away with "the debris of Cold War dogma," dating to the declaration of a state of emergency at the outbreak of the Korean War in 1950.

A December 7, 1969, editorial in *The Washington Post*, titled "Mathias Bids Congress Rise Again," credited the first-term senator's bold approach to bolstering congressional authority: "A freshman senator from Maryland has initiated what may become the most novel action of the 91st Congress—and one of the most momentous."

His independent streak irritated the Nixon White House—he was never invited to the residence. Yet Republicans and Democrats praised his bipartisan spirit and low-key demeanor. "He's always got that cherubic smile and twinkle in his eyes," one conservative GOP senator commented. "He doesn't take himself so seriously as to be ponderous."

Mathias remained a vocal critic of the war in Vietnam during the Nixon administration, working with liberal Republicans and many Democrats to urge de-escalation, withdrawal deadlines and an end to the bombing.

He drew national headlines when Nixon sent troops into Laos. "Nixon is subverting the will of Congress with this military escalation in Laos," the freshman senator declared in February 1970. The president is turning Laos into "an arena for the repetition of the mistakes of [Vietnam]."

His criticism was undergirded by a growing interest in taking legislative action to curtail the emergency powers of a president.

He co-chaired a special Senate committee on emergency powers with Senator Frank Church (D–ID) in 1973 that identified 580 actions by Congress dating back to 1933 that granted a president far-reaching emergency authority.

Mathias was a strong advocate for the War Powers Act passed by Congress in late 1973 and, subsequently, over Nixon's veto. The act requires notification to Congress of any commitment of U.S. forces into armed conflict within 48 hours and places a 60-day limit on their presence. It has been widely disregarded by several presidents.

Mathias had more to do with passage of legislation in 1973 that ended a series of "national emergencies" dating to 1917 that had been used by many presidents to wage war without constraint. Still in his first term, Mathias joined forces with Senator Adlai Stevenson III (D–IL) to hold hearings and pass legislation that repealed congressional grants of authority to presidents—that had turned the Senate, Mathias argued, into little more than "a constitutional relic."

* * *

Politically, Mathias remained a thorn in the side of the GOP establishment. He had been an independent-minded Republican from the earliest stages of his career.

In 1964, he surprised friends by voting for Barry Goldwater, the conservative Arizona senator who was the party's nominee against President Johnson. In 1968 and 1972, he was cagey about openly backing Nixon and Vice President Agnew, the latter a former Maryland governor who was forced to resign in 1973 for corruption. But he did call for their election.

Right-wing Republicans who were gunning to defeat Mathias were caught off guard in July 1972 when the White House sent their national security adviser Henry Kissinger to back Mathias at a large fund-raising dinner in Maryland. Kissinger said the administration hoped Mathias "will be with us for a long time."

That strong show of support flabbergasted GOP conservatives. Not only had Mathias been an outspoken foe of the Nixon administration on Southeast Asia but he had also voted against two Nixon nominees for the Supreme Court and had been sharply critical as far back as 1969 of Nixon's "Southern strategy," which exploited racial issues, crime and student unrest.

Watergate: Coming Close to Dictatorship

Senator Mathias was one of the first Republicans to back an investigation of the break-in at the Democratic party headquarters at the Watergate complex in 1972. He never let up as the scandal unfolded.

Still in his first term in October 1972, he was the only GOP member on the Senate Judiciary Committee to support subpoenas of White House staffers to get to the bottom of the Watergate break-in and fix responsibility.

He demanded full disclosure of all documents, tape recordings and any information related to the break-in and the subsequent cover-up. He charged that the Nixon White House was "trampling on truth and the rule of law."

Drawing upon American history in a long speech on the Senate floor just before Christmas 1973, Mathias called for major changes in U.S. governance, including in campaign finance, limits on the powers of the CIA and FBI and empowerment of local government across the country.

In that speech, he accused the Nixon administration of "authoritarian" rule and "government by cabal"—and in an interview after the speech he said, "No one knows how close we came to a dictatorship in the last four or five years."

The following comment Mathias made during Watergate should have resonance today, when so many Republicans have ignored the rule of law to support Donald Trump's desperate and coup-like bid to overturn a democratic election:

> There have been actions over the past few years that have caused some in positions of power and responsibility to forget that the highest loyalty of an American public servant is not to any personality, whether he be a President or a general or a senator; nor is it to any organization, department, agency or party. His first loyalty is to the law of the land built upon constitutional foundations by Thomas Jefferson, George Washington, Alexander Hamilton, George Mason, and other great men of our revolutionary past.

Upon Nixon's resignation in August 1974, the senator didn't even mention Nixon's name in a comment for the press but focused on the need for the country to heal its wounds and help now–President Gerald Ford restore faith in government.

Mathias' most immediate task following Nixon's departure was his own reelection. His strong opposition to Nixon and long support for social reforms and civil rights secured easy victories in both the GOP primary and the general election. In the latter, he defeated Barbara Mikulski, a formidable young city councilwoman and social activist. (Mikulski would win election to the House two years later and succeed Mathias when he retired in 1986.)

* * *

Mathias' Senate voting record seemed far more like a Democrat's than a Republican's. During his first term in 1973, for example, his rating from the liberal Americans for Democratic Action was the highest of any Republican. This pattern was consistent throughout Mathias' Senate career.

Mathias flirted with the possibility of running for president as an independent in late 1975 and early 1976, mostly to stop the cannibalization of his own party. He was motivated to block the favorite of the Republican right, California governor Ronald Reagan. Mathias charged then-incumbent Republican president Ford with kowtowing to the GOP right wing, and he didn't mince words as he explored a GOP primary run for president and then a third-party bid. He lambasted Ford in January 1976, noting that Ford's recent State of the Union Address completely ignored the plight of cities and the looming default of New York City. "Unfortunately, urban rot is not visible from the windows of Air Force One," Mathias said. He had support from influential Americans. James Reston, *The New York Times* columnist, wrote in 1975 of his despair that "the best and the strongest" senators such as Mathias were not more seriously considered worthy candidates for president.

Mathias was an equal opportunity critic, enthusiastically scorching Democrats as well. He attacked both Democratic and Republican presidential candidates for failing to back programs to address poverty and racial discrimination. "We must keep our priorities clear," he said. "Social programs aimed at alleviating the problems of the poor, the sick and the unsheltered—the vulnerable members of our society—must be and can be supported." He ultimately backed off his presidential quest. His chances of success were slim, he hated raising campaign funds, and he'd come from a long line of Republicans.

Mathias served on the Senate Committee on the District of Columbia and played a major role in establishing Home Rule for D.C. He was also key in the effort to create the C&O Canal National Park.

He never let up in his push to curtail the influence of money in politics. His departing remarks on the floor of the Senate in October 1986 captured the intensity he felt: "The extravagant financial demands of political campaigns and the accompanying pressure to yield to special interests constitute nothing less than a crisis of liberty." He introduced legislation to reform the campaign finance system in the early 1970s. He wanted to put a legal cap on individual and corporate campaign contributions, have public financing of campaigns and greater disclosure of funds raised. Many of these issues were addressed as a part of a comprehensive reform package that passed Congress in 1974, which Mathias had a hand in shaping.

Wearing his good government hat, he resisted efforts to further politicize the executive branch. Maryland is heavily populated with civil servants, and he was highly protective of them. (In the mid–1970s, the state had 132,000 federal employees.) In 1978, he attacked President Carter's Civil Service reorganization proposal to add more political positions, charging that "it invited political and personal favoritism and should be rejected in Congress." Throughout his time in office, Mathias was particularly disturbed by the appointment of political supporters of a president—Republican or Democrat—to ambassadorships and foreign policy positions for which they were not well qualified. He was a strong supporter of expertise in the U.S. Foreign Service.

Mathias was frequently out of step with the Republican Party—but his national leadership on civil rights, women's rights, anti-poverty and environmental programs resonated with Marylanders. He always looked out for the impact of legislation on his state.

One of the best illustrations of Mathias' courage and tenacity was his work to restore the Chesapeake Bay. He spent his entire career in the Senate pushing the cleanup of the Bay, the country's largest estuary. He used his seat on the Senate Appropriations Committee to fund a $27 million study of the Bay from 1975 to 1983. After the release of the study, which produced evidence that the Bay was dying, Mathias engineered the effort to get the conservative, anti-environmental Reagan White House to provide $40 million over four years for an EPA-led, federal-state partnership to begin to restore the Bay. The Bay cleanup effort became a model for the nation.

He singled out his work on the Bay as one of his finest accomplishments. "The Chesapeake Bay effort will, I hope, have a profound impact on the life of the Bay and the lives of the people who live around the Bay," he said.

As a member of the Senate Appropriations Committee throughout much of the 1970s, Mathias could wield a great deal of power to get projects and programs that helped Maryland and its institutions. And because Appropriations held the purse strings for the federal government, federal agencies had to pay attention to Mathias' requests.

For example, the highly colorful, never-take-no-for-an-answer mayor of Baltimore, William Donald Schaefer (later governor), was constantly nipping at his heels, asking for help. Mathias not only voted for national programs that would help the people of Baltimore but he also worked to improve the city's waterfront at a critical juncture, securing federal funds to develop the Inner Harbor. Mathias had the chutzpah to push through the Senate (and Barbara Mikulski later got it passed in the House, so it became law) a bill that designated the Baltimore Aquarium as the "national aquarium," enhancing Baltimore's attraction as a tourist destination.

On the national stage, he was a strong supporter of programs to help urban areas such as Baltimore. He even took Democratic president Jimmy Carter to task in 1977, calling Carter's urban budget "just as stingy" as those offered in the Nixon and Ford administrations. Mathias placed a high priority on jobs in urban areas, especially for Marylanders, and on boosting Maryland's local economies.

Mathias also worked to convert unused federal facilities to civilian use. Ever mindful of his constituents, he launched a two-year campaign with others in the Maryland delegation to save the army's Fort Detrick in Frederick, Maryland, an abandoned site for chemical and biological warfare activities. He got the backing of the Nixon White House to convert it into a national cancer and medical research center.

Mathias fought hard for the state and its localities, but he could not do this alone. Many of these efforts to protect Maryland's natural resources, its institutions and the federal facilities in the state would not have been successful without the full weight of the Maryland congressional delegation. Mathias was dean of the delegation for most of his Senate career, even though it was comprised mostly of Democrats.

Mathias also worked closely with his fellow senators from neighboring Virginia on regional issues. He fought for Washington Metro funding, to protect federal employees, and most importantly, to clean up the Chesapeake Bay. He especially worked closely with his friend and Virginia GOP senator John Warner on these issues and to establish the Vietnam Veterans Memorial in the late 1970s and early 1980s.

Mathias led the long effort to honor veterans of the war, overcoming fierce opposition from conservatives and a powerful appointee in the Reagan administration who came close to derailing the project because of their objections to the memorial's design.

In another struggle that divided the nation, Mathias was out front on women's rights. In May 1980 he helped lead a march with Bella Abzug and

Gloria Steinem with 50,000 women parading through Chicago's lakefront Grant Park in support of the Equal Rights Amendment. It was meaningful enough for him that he displayed a picture of the event in his Senate office. Not long afterward, at the Republican convention in late July, he broke ranks with his fellow party members by urging the GOP to reaffirm its traditional support of the Equal Rights Amendment, despite President Reagan's opposition. "A GOP retreat on the issue would suggest that the party of freedom no longer deserves its name," Mathias said.

* * *

Mathias generally supported President Carter, especially in foreign policy, voting for, while criticizing aspects of, the Democratic president's Panama Canal treaties. He also supported Carter's consequential push for peace between Israel and Egypt, arms sales to Israel and major Arab nations, the normalizing of relations with China and arms control initiatives.

The Iran hostage crisis—which contributed to Carter's loss to Reagan in the 1980 election—posed a delicate challenge for Republicans. Unlike other party leaders, the GOP's top members of Congress were careful not to exploit the foreign crisis. Mathias sharply criticized the intelligence

President Reagan, Vice President George H.W. Bush and Senator Mathias in the Oval Office, 1983 (Mathias Family).

failures that led to a misreading of the depth of unrest in Iran, but he did not go on the attack against Carter. His campaign for reelection to a third term was well-financed, and his popularity in Maryland was reflected in the fact that his name appeared on many Democratic club ballots along with Mr. Carter's. He won handily.

* * *

Mathias' most severe ideological clash with a sitting president came during the Reagan administration.

When Reagan became president in 1981, his goal was to fundamentally diminish the role of the federal government. Reagan's mantra was that government was the problem, not the solution.

White House budgets drastically curtailed or eliminated important social, economic and environmental programs. The Senate then was in Republican control, but Mathias and other moderate to liberal Republicans, the so-called Gang of Six, pushed back. Together with Democrats, they helped water down or defeat many of Reagan's most draconian budget proposals. In contrast to today, bipartisan coalitions were commonly forged to block controversial proposals or to promote good policies.

Senator Mathias (right) and Senator Joseph Biden (center) discussing legislation (photograph by Stanford Barouh).

One of the most dramatic and revealing instances of Senator Mathias' independence and willingness to stand alone in pursuit of his beliefs came in Reagan's first term during a popular groundswell of support—in both parties—for "tough on crime" legislation.

With Republicans now in control of the U.S. Senate for the first time in decades, bills mandating strict sentencing and mass incarceration were pushed by both the GOP and Democrats—in the latter case led by Senator Joe Biden.

Mathias argued vigorously against the bills' harshest provisions, predicting the "Violent Crime and Drug Enforcement Act" would lead to terrible overcrowding in federal prisons—which did happen. He was the lone senator to oppose passage of the bill, 95–1.

Senator Mathias frequently clashed with the Reagan White House on foreign policy as well.

Even in the early stages of the Reagan presidency, Mathias took a bold step in criticizing the outsized influence of ethnic lobbies on American foreign policy in a long article in the magazine *Foreign Affairs*. He specifically cited "the potent Israel lobby"—as well as Greek and Irish groups—for exerting extraordinary pressure that often proves "harmful to the public interest."

"Presidents from Wilson to Carter (and Reagan will too) confronted the dilemma of citizens who couple loyalty to America with bonds of affection for one foreign country or another," he wrote.

The article triggered broad criticism from Israel's powerful lobby in the United States and from many Maryland Jews, who had been strong supporters of the senator. Now in his third term, he declined to join a discussion of the article, but his candor on a sensitive topic did increase criticism of him.

Early in the Reagan administration, Mathias focused much of his energies on the two issues that concerned him the most: nuclear arms control and Middle East peace.

He regularly took issue with President Reagan's approach to nuclear arms issues, and he could do it with a flair for striking rhetoric. Opposing a nuclear freeze as unrealistic, he said the United States should break the idea of a freeze into "many individual ice cubes—usable, manageable, practical steps that can cool the arms race."

Given his eye-witness experience of seeing the devastation of Hiroshima at the end of World War II, Senator Mathias remained a steadfast advocate of limiting and reducing nuclear weapons—and all weapons of mass destruction.

In his first term as a senator, he led an effort to brake the arms race with the Soviet Union by pushing hard to extend the Nuclear Test Ban

Treaty to stop underground testing unless all parties agreed to mandatory on-site inspections. The Soviets, with only one-third of the nuclear warheads of the United States at the time, opposed such limitations.

Mathias was a Senate observer at subsequent Strategic Arms Limitation Talks (SALT II) in 1977, and he drew praise from Democratic majority leader Mike Mansfield for being "in the forefront of this particular issue."

He opposed Reagan's space-based "Star Wars" program, and, returning from his fourth trip to Moscow, he relayed Soviet determination to delay progress in all nuclear talks until the administration dropped its Star Wars build-up.

On the Middle East, Mathias remained pragmatic and centrist, supporting arms sales to both Israel and moderate Arab nations but critical of Israel's settlement expansion and its intervention in Lebanon.

When several U.S. Marines died in Lebanon after Reagan ordered a peacekeeping force into the country, Mathias was an outspoken leader of efforts to force the administration to invoke the War Powers Act—which he had had a hand in establishing. While opposing outright withdrawal, he pressed for a six-month limit to the engagement if the administration balked.

"U.S. forces have been engaged in hostilities," he said in a Senate speech in late September 1983. "We have suffered casualties. It is clear that the War Powers Act applies. The Congress has a constitutional role, and that role has to be recognized."

One month later, 241 Marines and 58 French soldiers were killed in the terrorist bombing of the Marine barracks in Beirut.

Despite repeated assertions that U.S. forces would stay to try to restore order, President Reagan ordered the withdrawal of U.S. troops three months later—without ever retaliating against the Lebanese Shiite and Syrian actors behind the attack.

Second Reagan Term

It was a cruel twist of fate. It fell to Mathias as chairman of the Senate Rules Committee to head the committee that organized President Reagan's second inauguration. And it was so cold on January 20, 1985—7 degrees Fahrenheit, with a severe wind chill—that the public ceremony had to be moved indoors to the Capitol Rotunda.

Mathias was chair of the Rules Committee only because Senator Thurmond (R–SC) had turned his back on the Armed Services Committee to take the chairmanship of the more powerful Judiciary Committee to block Mathias, the bane of the Reaganites, from assuming its leadership.

Reagan, the oldest person to become president until Joe Biden, was sworn in by Supreme Court Chief Justice Warren E. Burger.

* * *

Speculation mounted in 1985 that Mathias might not run for a fourth term in 1986. He did not look vulnerable politically despite the growing irritation of the Republican establishment—now very much in the Reagan mold. But he made it official on September 25, 1985, becoming the fourth GOP senator to announce retirement.

His reasons have long remained a bit of a puzzle. Speculation includes his strong distaste for campaign fund-raising, the growing antagonism toward him from the GOP right, and the Israeli lobby's irritation with his 1981 *Foreign Affairs* article. Perhaps all three.

Also, several of his closest liberal and moderate Republican colleagues—Jacob Javits of New York, Clifford Case of New Jersey and Charles "Chuck" Percy of Illinois—had been defeated in recent years. He also occasionally mused that it might be time to make some "real money"—and many law firms were ready to sign him up.

His announcement that September was not very revealing. Expressing his frustration that he couldn't accomplish what he wished, he said, "The season has arrived to shift to a new field of activity."

* * *

Once freed of political concerns, the senator from Frederick was able to spend even more of his remaining time in the Senate on deep engagement in foreign affairs and national security.

He devoted much of the last 18 months of his Senate career to work on the Senate Foreign Relations Committee, especially Middle East peace, arms control issues, energy concerns and sanctions legislation against the apartheid regime in South Africa.

Since he no longer had to worry about missing Senate votes, he traveled frequently. He was president of NATO's Parliamentary Assembly and that meant meetings in Europe, Turkey and San Francisco. In the spring of 1986, he devoted three weeks to an arduous trip through the key nations of the Middle East, where he was treated with respect by heads of state and the most senior officials of Saudi Arabia, Syria, Jordan, Israel and Egypt. Kings, prime ministers and foreign secretaries shared sensitive intelligence and assessments with him and two top aides. The energy minister of Saudi Arabia flew him over the Ras Tanura oilfields in the midst of the on-going Iraq-Iran war, and the defense minister of Egypt put a plane at his disposal to tour the Nile and the striking ruins at Luxor—a typical perk of a senior senator's foreign travel.

With assistance from his staff, he contributed long and substantive trip reports to the Foreign Relations Committee, plus op-ed articles on major issues such as the search for peace in the Middle East, nuclear arms reduction negotiations and the U.S.-Soviet proxy conflict in Africa.

He played a leading role in shaping a tough but balanced set of sanctions against the White minority regime in South Africa. The sanctions legislation was vetoed by President Reagan, but 30 of the 53 GOP senators joined Mathias and 47 Democrats to overturn Reagan's veto at the height of the president's popularity. Senator Mitch McConnell of Kentucky and a number of "red state" Midwestern senators were among the 31 Republicans to join the rejection of their own party's president in an historic display of bipartisanship in the national interest—one that would be unthinkable in the GOP of the 21st century.

* * *

The summer of 1986 was dominated by the unfolding Iran-contra scandal—the reckless scheme in which senior Reagan officials secretly sold arms to Iran in hopes of freeing American hostages but also to gain funds to give to the Nicaraguan *Contras*—which had been specifically prohibited by congressional legislation. Eleven officials were convicted in the scandal, but the president, Vice President George H.W. Bush and other senior leaders dodged the bullet. After denying the facts for months, Reagan finally conceded in a nationally televised speech that "a strategic opening to Iran deteriorated into trading arms for hostages."

Reminiscing in 1986 on his time in office, as the scandal dominated television screens across the country, Senator Mathias spoke out bluntly and blamed the Iran affair "on a lack of respect for the Constitution."

As his formal retirement approached, the senator spoke frequently about the principles and values that had guided him throughout his career in public office.

"No one has reverenced the Constitution more than I," he told an interviewer in December 1986. "If you are willing to apply the Constitution as it is, the First Amendment, the Fourth Amendment, the 14th Amendment, all of the really great monuments of constitutional law, then there isn't much room for ideology."

He said he would regret leaving when there were so many critical challenges facing the country, both economically and abroad. But, he added, "I am leaving the way you should leave a party—while you're still having fun."

Given the growing strength of the right wing in his party, it was clear that Mathias was no longer having much fun or satisfaction. In a candid interview with Alan Crawford in *Warfield's* magazine in late 1986, the senator directed some blame at himself and fellow GOP moderates. "The ultraconservative wing of the party has been allowed to gain power only because of the weakness of the moderates—and I have to plead guilty to that. We moderates get so entranced with the business of governing and get so immersed in the day-to-day operations of the Congress and the administration that we do not pay close attention to party affairs. We tend to leave that to 'others.'"

Crawford, author of the book *Thunder of the Right*, offered a succinct and striking assessment of Mac Mathias in that essay, not only by noting that the senator's preference for driving a beat-up old Buick station wagon helped imbue a public image that he was, despite his establishment roots, "just folks," but in a broader summary of his career. "Endowed with a sense of history, motivated more by an ethic of public service than personal striving, he has brought to his political career qualities of personal decency and independence of judgment which have served him—and the country—well at a time when Congress all too often seems dominated by hustlers and opportunists."

People, he quoted the senator as adding, "yearn for simple answers as life becomes more complex. Simplistic rhetoric that has been offered by some Republicans has promised easy answers to complicated problems of modern life. But life is just not that simple."

* * *

Nine months after the end of his Senate career, Mathias joined the large international law firm of Jones, Day, Reavis and Pogue. He also agreed to teach at the Johns Hopkins University as the first Milton Eisenhower Professor of Public Affairs.

In 1992, he was appointed by a federal judge to oversee the dissolution of First American Bankshares, a bank that was ensnared in the collapse of the huge Bank of Credit and Commerce International (BCCI), a Middle Eastern-Pakistani–owned bank regarded as having operated the largest money-laundering racket in history. Mathias had been a member of First American's board since 1987.

One of the most significant activities of Senator Mathias' post–Senate career was his involvement with the Diplomacy Center Foundation (DCF), a non-profit organization that has partnered with the U.S. Department of State to build a museum at the department dedicated to American diplomacy.

Mathias served as the first chair of the DCF board of directors from 1999 until his death in 2010. A 20,000-square-foot glass pavilion that houses exhibit hall 1 and the Founding Ambassadors Concourse was opened in 2017, and an addition is planned to house two more exhibit halls. The pavilion displays temporary exhibits and hosts a range of educational and public programs.

Ambassador Roman Popadiuk, president of DCF, said, "Senator Mathias' firm belief in the role of diplomacy in maintaining peace and furthering U.S. interests, as well as respect for the men and women who conduct that diplomacy, underscored his visionary dedication to build the museum."

In 2008 in another sign of his political independence, Mathias endorsed the Democratic candidate for president, Barack Obama, over GOP senator John McCain. In a *Washington Post* column, he wrote, "Obama promises a clean break from the recent past [Iraq war and financial meltdown of 2007–08] and tangible hope for a return to fiscal responsibility, economic security and true environmental stewardship."

His son, Robert Mathias, said his father's endorsement was a tough decision and was only partly a recognition of the historic moment. "He really liked John McCain, but felt that the vice-presidential choice [of Sarah Palin] was a sign of what was happening to the GOP. Also, he really felt that his time on the stage ought to be over."

Senator Mathias died on January 25, 2010.

I. In the National Interest

Mathias and the Civil Rights Movement

MICHAEL R. KLIPPER *and*
JOHN HOUGH, JR.

Charles McC. Mathias, Jr., was widely known and respected for his work on a variety of issues, domestic and foreign. But he is best known and admired for his championing of civil rights and voting rights for all Americans. He was guided by two fundamental principles: an unyielding commitment to advancing racial equality and an adherence to the founding tenets of the "Party of Lincoln." He is widely considered one of the political heroes of his generation. Legendary civil rights lawyer Joe Rauh called Mathias "the best Republican friend civil rights has had."[1]

Mathias was a lifelong Republican—perhaps more accurately, a lifelong Lincoln Republican. To Mathias, "[t]he Republican Party ... was the bulwark of the Union and was the shield for the rights of individual citizens."[2] He was quick to remind people of his family's Republican lineage. His great-grandfather, Charles Trail, ran for the Maryland Senate from Frederick on the anti-slavery Republican ticket headed by the future president, Abraham Lincoln.

At the heart of the party's appeal to Mathias was the fact that from its inception in the 1850s and for a century thereafter, through the great civil rights and voting rights battles of the 1960s, the Republican Party was closely identified with the cause of racial equality and civil rights.

Mathias took pride in the fact that Republicans oversaw issuance of the Emancipation Proclamation and the adoptions of the 13th, 14th and 15th Amendments. He was also gratified that 100 years later, due to the efforts of many Republican members of the House and Senate, the Civil Rights Act of 1964 and the Voting Rights Act of 1965—perhaps the two most impactful laws of all time—bore a Republican imprimatur. Without members of the party of Lincoln, these laws would not have been enacted

35

or would have been dramatically weakened, as their predecessors—the 1957 and 1960 Civil Rights Acts—had been.

* * *

When Mathias launched his legal career in the 1950s, Maryland was a segregated state, very Southern in its treatment of its Black population. Jim Crow thrived. Black Marylanders suffered the inequities of segregation in schools, public accommodations, housing, restrooms, theaters, parks, libraries, public transportation, restaurants, lunch counters, shopping venues, beaches and swimming pools. As Mathias acknowledged years later, "Maryland remained a profoundly segregated state."

During those years, Maryland was also the site of a vigorous desegregation campaign led by civil rights activists in the state. It was also home to many iconic civil rights figures, all of whom were heroes to Mathias. Among them were Thurgood Marshall, renowned civil rights litigator and strategist and the first Black Supreme Court Justice, and Juanita Jackson Mitchell, the first Black woman to practice law in Maryland. Ms. Mitchell was the wife of another legendary figure in the civil rights movement, Clarence Mitchell, Jr., a partner of Mathias' in the effort to push Congress to enact civil rights and voting rights legislation.

Among politicians, two-time Baltimore mayor and two-time Maryland governor Republican Theodore McKeldin was a role model and inspiration to Mathias. While McKeldin was rightfully praised for such accomplishments as the building of the BWI Airport and initiating the revival of Baltimore's Inner Harbor, perhaps his greatest success was the example he set on the civil rights front for Mathias and so many others.

* * *

For years, the Frederick City Opera House, which operated as a movie theater and was home to the city council, was a segregated venue. In the late 1950s the orchestra and the first few rows of the balcony were "Whites only" and there were separate toilets for Whites and Blacks. Then Juanita Mitchell and the NAACP took legal action to desegregate the theater.

Ms. Mitchell had no inkling of how the young city attorney, Charles McC. Mathias, Jr., or the city would respond to the lawsuit. Ms. Mitchell was unaware that Mathias, who was born and raised in Frederick, was deeply troubled by the "really dreadful" racial inequities in Maryland and around the country. As Mathias said years later, "none of the landmark legislation that characterized the civil rights revolution of the sixties had yet been written, so the legal situation was not as clear as it may appear in retrospect." But while segregation was common in the life of Marylanders, Mathias sensed that "change was in the air."

According to Mrs. Mitchell, she was called by Mathias. He reported, "I had talked with the Mayor and City Council of Frederick, and they have agreed with me that we will enter a consent decree and desegregate the theatre in the City Opera House, which houses the City Council. They have agreed that that is right and just." The parties then entered into a consent decree that was adopted by the court, ending the matter. "No appeal, just a consent decree."[3]

Decades later, Mathias reflected on his respect for Mrs. Mitchell.

It may sound tame today in the wake of tremendous legal and social change, but it was a new and courageous act when Juanita brought the NAACP legal team to Frederick. Distances seemed greater in those days, and Frederick was a distinctly agricultural community deeply rooted

Juanita Jackson Mitchell, civil rights leader and the head of the NAACP in her Baltimore office (Baltimore Sun Media. All Rights Reserved).

in traditional ways of life. It was not an easy job to tackle, but Juanita never hesitated, and never showed any sign of weakness or doubt.[4]

During his years of legislative service, Mathias cast many votes in support of racial equality, but we suspect that one of the senator's most cherished votes did not occur in Washington, D.C. It took place in Annapolis, Maryland, when he voted aye in 1959 as a member of the Maryland House of Delegates on the resolution that finally put Maryland on record in favor of the ratification of the 14th Amendment to the U.S. Constitution.

The 14th Amendment was added to the Constitution in 1868 when it was adopted by the requisite number of states. Maryland had refused to ratify the amendment in 1867.

After years of lying dormant, the issue of Maryland's ratification of the amendment gained renewed attention in the mid–1950s. A few years before Mathias became a member of the House of Delegates, Harry A. Cole, the state's first Black senator, and later the first Black member of the state's highest court, launched a campaign to ratify the 14th Amendment, but his efforts were met with staunch opposition and were unsuccessful. Prospects for adoption soon improved as more Blacks were elected to the Maryland legislature.

Finally, the year Mathias joined the House of Delegates, 1959, 91 years after the 14th Amendment became part of our organic national law, Maryland ratified it. As one of those votes in favor of ratification, Mathias was proud to characterize himself as "one of the ratifiers of the Fourteenth Amendment."[5] His vote in favor of ratification was easy. He was well versed in the guarantees embedded in the amendment: (1) equal protection under the law, the most litigated part of the U.S. Constitution and the basis for such landmark Supreme Court decisions as *Brown v. Board of Education* (1954); (2) due process; and (3) citizenship for all persons born or naturalized in the United States. He knew that the amendment played an instrumental role in shaping our nation's commitment to civil rights and civil liberties.

* * *

Mathias arrived in Washington as a freshman congressman in 1961. It was a critical time in the civil rights movement. He seized the opportunity to establish his bona fides as a Lincoln Republican and advocate for racial equality. Mathias found himself deeply involved in the legislative battles that yielded the Civil Rights Act of 1964 and the Voting Rights Act of 1965.

After years of Southern Democrats frustrating efforts to enact civil rights laws, things began to change during President Eisenhower's second term. In 1957 and again in 1960, Congress passed and the president signed into law civil rights bills—the first to be enacted in 80 years. While watered down in final form and of limited practical consequence, these laws were nonetheless of symbolic value. They foreshadowed the seismic and groundbreaking legislative victories to come. As Joe Rauh wrote, "The 1957 bill, weak as it was, became the first step in the long journey to the great laws of the 1960's."

Calls for racial equality reverberated in the presidential election of 1960. Both candidates ran on party platforms that attacked racial discrimination in forceful terms designed to win support within the civil rights community. Despite John F. Kennedy's endorsement of the Democratic platform, his belief that pursuing racial equality was a moral imperative, and the critical role that the Black vote played in his 1960 election, Kennedy initially moved with some reluctance on civil rights legislation. His hesitancy was based primarily on political calculations: fear that adopting a strong civil rights stance could threaten key portions of his legislative agenda—including tax cuts and space exploration—and jeopardize his re-election in 1964. And, of course, there were daunting political hurdles in the way of enacting tough civil rights legislation.

Kennedy's caution frustrated civil rights advocates. It also prompted a group of House Republicans to move to fill the void. Representatives William McCulloch (R–OH), one of the great unsung heroes of the push for the Civil Rights Act of 1964 and longtime ranking member of the House Judiciary Committee, John Lindsay (R–NY), and Mathias introduced a comprehensive Republican civil rights bill on January 31, 1963. To Mathias, the introduction of the Republican bill "was the thing that stirred the Kennedy administration to finally get their bill drafted and introduced." The Democrats, according to Mathias, realized "that they were being outpaced."[6]

At the time the bill was introduced in the House, Lindsay acknowledged that "aside from the work of ranking member McCulloch," no one "worked more diligently" in the preparation of the 47-page bill than Mathias. When it was Mathias' turn to speak, he underscored both the importance to our forefathers of protecting civil rights and the historical role the Republican party had played in protecting those rights:

> Whether we call it liberty or civil rights, they are the principles for which this country sought its independence.... They [were] the principle[s] [upon which] the Republican Party was founded.... I am glad that this bill is going to be known as a Republican bill. I am glad ... that the Republican Party has seized the initiative on the question of preservation of liberty and the guarantee of civil rights.[7]

Ultimately, the Kennedy administration sent the Hill its own civil rights bill, which became the focus of the congressional debate. And Kennedy's team knew that passage of their bill would in large part rest on Republican votes. And when a comprehensive civil rights bill appeared to be on life support in mid–1963, an agreement between Representative McCulloch and the Kennedy administration revived the legislation and proved critical to eventual passage of the landmark Civil Rights Act of 1964.

McCulloch agreed to support a reasonable civil rights bill and convince other House Republicans to do so. He secured pledges from the administration that he would be allowed to approve any amendments to the bill and that, if the bill were passed by the House, it would not be emasculated in the Senate in order to appease Southern Democrats. The Kennedy administration also agreed to acknowledge publicly the key role played by the Republicans in supporting the legislation.

Mathias played a critical role during the House's consideration of the bill, H.R. 7152. Not surprisingly, he defended key provisions of the bill on the floor, particularly its hotly debated public accommodations language, Title II. Exhibiting a keen knowledge of English and American common law, he debunked the arguments that these provisions were an invasion of privacy and constituted a radical new theory: that an innkeeper must serve all members of the public. "[I]t is clear that the basic theory" undergirding the public accommodations language "is part of an ancient heritage of jurisprudence which continues as a dynamic force in our law today."[8]

The agreement held. It survived the tragic murder of John Kennedy and was adhered to by the Johnson administration. Senate proponents overcame a filibuster by Southern Democrats and the legislation was passed by both houses. President Johnson signed it into law on July 2, 1964.

Without Republican support, the 1964 Act would not have become law. Mathias was one of several House and Senate Republicans who deserve credit, but for Mathias, none played a more pivotal role than his mentor and hero, Representative McCulloch, a descendant of abolitionists. President Johnson dubbed McCulloch "the most important and powerful force" in the enactment of the bill. And Jackie Kennedy Onassis later told him, "I know you, more than anyone, were responsible for the civil rights legislation of the 1960's, particularly for the Civil Rights Act of 1964."[9]

* * *

Following passage of the 1964 Civil Rights Act, President Johnson believed that some time should pass to allow the country to digest the new law before Congress took up comprehensive voting rights legislation. But dramatic events, particularly in Selma, Alabama, altered his thinking and that of Congress and the American people.

The massive voter registration efforts and the horrific response of local law enforcement stunned the world and helped change history. At the height of the clashes in Selma, Mathias and 14 of his House colleagues traveled to that city to review reports of rampant voting discrimination. The delegation met with Dr. Martin Luther King. After this meeting, Mathias predicted "that a Republican voting rights proposal will be introduced as a result of this thing."

When he returned from Selma, he and some of his House colleagues, including Lindsay and Ogden Reid (R–NY), introduced a voting rights bill. It empowered the federal government to send in registrars to register prospective voters who had been denied the right to vote if there was found to be, in a particular area, a pattern of voting discrimination. In his introductory remarks, Mathias reminded his colleagues that more than seven years earlier the idea of authorizing federal registrars was put forth by a Republican, President Eisenhower's attorney general Herbert Brownell, Jr., and that the bill was intended to implement Brownell's suggestion.

Senator Mathias and President Johnson, April 11, 1968 (White House photo).

Two weeks later, on February 23, 1965, as the violence in Selma continued, Mathias and Senator Tom Kuchel (R–CA) organized a statement by a group of 32 Republicans that criticized the Johnson administration for its continuing refusal to announce publicly what form its promised voting rights legislation would take.

Then, on March 15, 1965, President Johnson told a joint session of Congress that the time had come. He told the nation, "we have already waited a hundred years and more. And the time for waiting is gone." Within days, a new comprehensive voting rights bill was introduced in the Senate and the House. Less than five months later, on August 6, 1965, President Johnson signed into law the Voting Rights Act of 1965.

The new law abandoned the case-by-case litigation model endorsed by the 1957, 1960 and 1964 Civil Rights Acts, which had failed to trigger any real uptick in minority voter registration. Congress was convinced that piecemeal lawsuits were time-consuming and expensive, typically took four years to complete, and even if successful were too often followed by a new discriminatory practice not barred by the prior adjudication or by defiance of the judicial decree. The bill relied in large part on a regulatory-oriented approach that required jurisdictions with a history of voting discrimination to petition the federal government for pre-approval of any new voting laws. This "preclearance" approach in Section 5 proved remarkably successful. To Mathias, "the fact that [by passing the Voting

Right Act] we actually got the Black voters into the voting booth transformed American politics more than any other single act."[10]

* * *

The stakes were high when Congress turned its attention to voting rights in 1981. The 1965 Act's special provisions, including the trigger for Section 5 preclearance, were due to expire in August 1982. Proponents of a new voting rights act were also committed to including in the bill a response to a 1980 Supreme Court decision, *Mobile v. Bolden*, that they argued curtailed dramatically Section 2 of the existing law, the Act's permanent tool for going to court to challenge discriminatory voting practices.

Prospects for enactment of such a new law in 1981 were uncertain. Approval by the Democrat-controlled House seemed quite likely, but the outlook in Senate was mixed at best. In January 1981, Republicans gained control of the Senate, and Strom Thurmond (R–SC), a long-time opponent of civil rights legislation, assumed the chairmanship of the Senate Judiciary Committee, the committee with jurisdiction over voting rights legislation. Further clouding the situation was uncertainty over where the conservative Reagan administration stood on a new voting rights bill. Under the umbrella of the Leadership Conference on Civil Rights, proponents of the legislation launched a massive lobbying campaign.

As a more than 20-year veteran of civil rights and voting rights legislative battles—particularly the successful efforts to enact the Voting Rights Act of 1965 and the 1970 and 1975 extensions of the 1965 law—Mathias was recognized as one of the leading advocates of civil rights in the Congress. He was the logical choice to serve as the lead sponsor in the Senate of the bill to renew and amend the 1965 Act. He assumed that role with tenacity and enthusiasm.

Twice in the 97th Congress, Mathias—with his long-term ally on social justice and civil rights Ted Kennedy (D–MA)—introduced legislation to extend and amend the Voting Rights Act. The second, S. 1992, was identical to the bill approved overwhelmingly by the House in October 1981. Among the key provisions were a 10-year extension of the Act's special provisions, including preclearance, and a response to *Mobile v. Bolden*. It was the latter provision that dominated the Senate's consideration of S. 1992.

The majority in *Bolden* had ruled that voting discrimination cases required proof of "discriminatory intent," a standard that civil rights activists argued negated much of the effectiveness of Section 2. Proponents sought to offset *Bolden* with adoption of a test based on a totality of circumstances that "result" in the denial of the right to vote, a test that did not require proof of a discriminatory intent. In a tense hearing in February 1982 before the Senate Judiciary Subcommittee on the Constitution, senators Mathias and Kennedy defended and debated the results-test language with subcommittee chairman Orrin Hatch (R–UT).

When the time arrived for him to testify before Hatch's subcommittee, Mathias left his seat on the dais and went to the witness table to deliver his remarks and answer questions. By doing so, he appeared to step away from his position as a senator and committee member to assume a role as a defender and advocate of voting rights legislation.

Ultimately, a compromise on Section 2 was offered by Senator Robert Dole (R–KS) and supported by Mathias, Kennedy, the civil rights community and eventually the Reagan administration. The Dole language was adopted by the committee and the revised bill was sent to the Senate, where Mathias served as floor manager. The Senate approved the bill on June 18 by an 85–8 vote, and President Reagan signed it into law on June 29, 1982.

The 1982 bill strengthened Section 2 and relaxed the terms under which a jurisdiction could "bailout" from coverage under Section 5. But

(From left) NAACP president Benjamin Hooks, Senator Howard Baker, Representative Walter Fauntroy, Senator Mathias, Coretta Scott King, Senator Bob Dole, SCLC president Joseph Lowery and Representative John Conyers, Jr., celebrate the establishment of the Martin Luther King holiday, October 19, 1983 (Mathias Family).

most remarkably, the new law extended the act's preclearance provisions for 25 years. Passage of the new law was a major accomplishment of Mathias's civil rights–based endeavor.

Mathias continued to be an advocate of civil rights and voting rights long after his retirement from the Senate. In 2005, key sections of the Voting Rights Act of 1965 were once again set to expire, including the one that triggered preclearance. For the fourth time, Congress undertook the task of extending those sections. To assist Congress in documenting the need to extend the provisions, civil rights groups established the National Commission on the Voting Rights Act. The commission named Mathias its honorary chair.

Upon receiving notification of his new role, Mathias extolled the importance of the 1965 Act. "The Voting Rights Act was really the whole core of the civil rights movement. It made a tremendous improvement," Mathias said. "There was a new recognition of black citizenship." Asked about the commission's investigation, Mathias declared, "We're having these hearings to establish the record that there is a need [to renew these provisions] ... I think the record will speak for itself."[11]

Both the commission's findings and Congress agreed with Mathias' prediction. Congress overwhelmingly approved the 2006 Voting Rights Amendments and Reauthorization Act and President George W. Bush signed it into law in July 2006. The representatives of the commission testified before Congress on the need for the 2006 bill and the commission report was cited repeatedly in the House Judiciary Committee's legislative report.

Then, in 2013, three years after Mathias's death, the Supreme Court, by a narrow 5–4 vote, disagreed. In *Shelby County v. Holder*, the court ruled unconstitutional the formula that determined which jurisdictions were covered by Section 5's preclearance requirements, rendering Section 5 inoperative unless Congress updated the coverage formula. It has not, and preclearance remains dormant.

* * *

Senator Mathias remained engaged in the battle for voting rights until the end of his life.

In both 2006 and 2007, while suffering more obviously from Parkinson's disease, Mathias made trips to Capitol Hill to voice his support for major voting rights legislation.

As chair of the House Judiciary Committee, Representative James Sensenbrenner, a strong backer of voting rights back to the early 1980s, had sponsored the 2006 voting rights bill, and Mathias was determined to show his appreciation for his dedication to the issue by visiting the congressman to thank him. A year later, he went to the Senate Judiciary Committee to lend his personal support to a bill, S. 453, the Deceptive Practices and Voter Intimidation Act of 2007. The legislation, introduced by senators Barack Obama (D–IL) and Charles Schumer (D–NY) and backed by Senator Ben Cardin (D–MD), was aimed at deterring misinformation on the time and place of elections and voter eligibility requirements.

Senator Cardin made note of Mathias's appearance, stating, "Senator Mathias wanted to be here today. He knew what the hearing was about and … it was not easy for him to physically get here today."

Among others who spoke of Mathias' presence was Senator Obama, who thanked him for coming to the hearing and for his statement in support of the bill.

* * *

With the 2008 presidential election, Mathias faced a "difficult" decision: to vote for John McCain, whom he had known for more than a quarter of a century, or for Barack Obama, who was making history as the first Black candidate for the presidency. In a guest column in *The Washington Post*, Mathias declared his support for Obama. He did so "with a sense of the historic significance of the choice before us all."

Mathias made clear that the decision was a close one, in part because of his family's past history of supporting Republican candidates for president since Lincoln's election in 1860. He recalled how he astounded many of his friends and supporters by voting for Barry Goldwater "despite disagreeing with many of his views and despite his lack of support in my congressional district." But Mathias' long involvement in the civil rights arena played a decisive part in his decision on the 2008 election. He acknowledged that

> the fact that he is also a Black American adds special significance for me as someone who was witness to and participated in at least a part of the past century's discourse on civil rights. Throughout my career in public office, I was involved in the effort to come to terms with our country's troubled history of race relations. I am proud to have helped enact several of the landmark civil rights laws that have been the cornerstones of our national response to the inequities perpetuated by racism. This is a moment in our national life that could scarcely have been contemplated at the beginning of my career, and one that I believe our country should savor.[12]

Mathias did not live long enough to witness much of the Obama presidency. He died 16 months after his endorsement. He was 87.

Notes

1. https://www.nytimes.com/1986/10/06/U.S./washington-talk-still-a-distinctive-voice-but-soon-an-echo.html.

2. https://cnsmaryland.org/1999/04/23/former-senator-looks-back-on-congress-and-doesnt-like-what-he-sees/.

3. https://msa.maryland.gov/megafile/msa/speccol/sc3500/sc3520/002000/002087/pdf/mathias_tribute.pdf.

4. https://digitalcommons.law.umaryland.edu/cgi/viewcontent.cgi?article=2872&context=mlr.

5. https://digitalcommons.law.umaryland.edu/cgi/viewcontent.cgi?article=2707&context=mlr.

6. https://www.emkinstitute.org/resources/charles-mathias-oral-history.

7. 88th Congress, Congressional Record, January 31, 1963, p. 1568.

8. 88th Congress, Congressional Record, February 1, 1964, pp. 1601–1602.

9. https://www.politico.com/magazine/story/2014/03/the-movers-behind-the-civil-rights-act-105216/.

10. https://www.emkinstitute.org/resources/charles-mathias.

11. https://thebaynet.com/senator-says-civil-rights-for-minorities-need-to-be-protected-html/.

12. https://www.washingtonpost.com/wp-dyn/content/article/2008/10/27/AR200810
2702407.html.

Saving the Bay

Monica Healy

When Mac Mathias was a little boy in the 1920s and 1930s, he loved riding in the family car on the *John M. Dennis*, the wide, double-ended ferry that travelled back and forth across the Chesapeake Bay long before a bridge was built to connect Annapolis with the Eastern Shore. Once on board, he'd jump out and race around the deck and imagine all the creatures underneath him—"the crabs, the oysters, the rockfish, all the rest," he recalled years later. It was the beginning of a lifelong love affair that culminated in the 1970s with his campaign to save the Bay from becoming a dead sea.

The Chesapeake Bay is the largest estuary in the United States, the third largest such body of water in the world. It's huge but shallow, about 200 miles long, from less than three miles wide where it begins in eastern Maryland to a 30-mile-wide bulge not far north of where it joins the Atlantic Ocean amid the Virginia capes. In about a quarter of its reach, someone six feet tall could wade without ever being completely submerged. It drains an enormous watershed that stretches as far north as Cooperstown, New York, and for centuries it was the source of an astonishing profusion of marine life, including crabs said to be big enough to feed four men and oysters the size of horses' hooves. Imagine *those* crowding the plate at your favorite seafood restaurant. Sadly, though, imagine is all you can do—crabs and oysters that big are long gone.

By the time Mathias was a first term U.S. senator in the early 1970s, the Bay he'd come to love as a boy was in frightening decline. Fish, oysters, crabs and waterfowl were disappearing. The once sparkling water had been turned murky by industrial discharge, raw sewage and farm runoff. No one seemed to know exactly how severe or far-reaching the problem was, have the necessary hard evidence of what was causing it, or, worse, have any plan for dealing with it. So Mathias set out on another boat trip to see for himself and to draw press and political attention to the unfolding disaster.

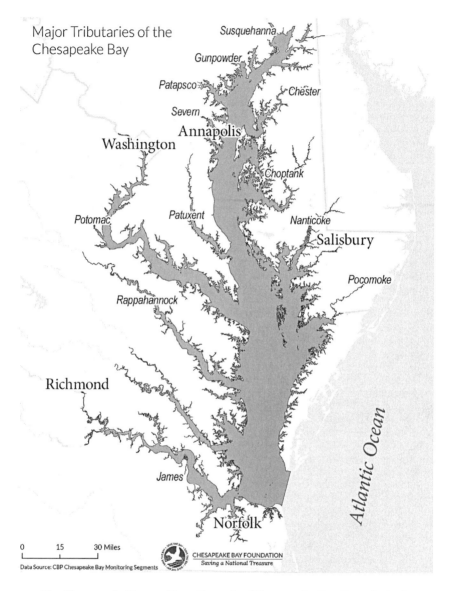

Major Tributaries of the
Chesapeake Bay

Susquehanna

Gunpowder

Patapsco

Chester

Severn

Annapolis

Washington

Choptank

Potomac

Patuxent

Nanticoke

Salisbury

Pocomoke

Rappahannock

Richmond

James

Norfolk

Atlantic Ocean

0   15   30 Miles

Data Source: CBP Chesapeake Bay Monitoring Segments

CHESAPEAKE BAY FOUNDATION
Saving a National Treasure

The Chesapeake Bay and its tributaries (Chesapeake Bay Foundation).

As the *Miss Afton IV*, a friend's yacht, pulled out of the Port of Baltimore in a driving rain in June 1973, Mathias and his family could see the huge industrial plants well known to be dumping contaminated wastewater and pollutants such as chromium into the harbor. Industry was the most obvious cause of the Bay's decline, but it was hardly the only culprit or the largest.

Mathias and Eastern Shore waterman Russell "Steamboat" Morris, 1980 (Mathias Family).

During the five-day trip, which went up the Bay's western shore and down the eastern shore, Mathias talked with farmers, watermen, researchers, businessmen, and state and local officials—anyone who knew anything about what was going on.[1]

They all confirmed what he could see himself. Municipal waste pipes were spewing sewage, farms were spreading chemicals that rain washed into the water, and industrial pollutants were poisoning the Bay at alarming rates. Ordinary people were adding to the damage every day through common practices such as the use of phosphate detergents.

The once beautiful Bay was becoming a hellscape. "There was a consensus among the people I talked to," he recalled in a speech years later, "that if this pollution continued unchecked, the oysters, crabs, shad, rockfish, striped bass, and the hundreds of other species that once abounded in the Bay would decline until there were simply no more to catch. The water would gradually become fatal to marine life, and the cancerous patches of dead sea bottom that had begun to appear in areas where the pollution was the worst would spread until they covered virtually the entire Bay floor—an environmental disaster of unimaginable proportions."[2]

Absolutely no one who could stop it was doing anything about it. It wasn't even on most government radar screens. That, Mathias knew, had to change.

* * *

I was fortunate to work on two of the senator's signature issues—the restoration of the Bay and creation of a memorial to Vietnam veterans. Both went to his core. He loved being outdoors, and he wanted to protect the land and the water and reverse the degradation he saw so plainly. And as a World War II veteran, he knew first-hand the awful cost of battle, and even though he'd opposed the Vietnam War, he could put himself in the shoes of the vets who fought in it yet were so badly treated once they got home.

With the benefit of decades of hindsight, both projects seem like no-brainers. But when the efforts began, they weren't obvious at all, and there was nothing easy about either of them. The campaign to involve the federal government in helping clean the Bay ran into a stone wall of conservative Republican conviction that such an effort would be nothing but wasteful pork barrel spending. The Vietnam memorial enraged opponents who thought the monument's now widely beloved design was a repudiation of the war and its veterans.

The way Mathias fought for both exemplified his best characteristics: fearlessness in the face of fierce opposition, a good natured but adamant refusal to back down, and cleverness at gradually gathering support and out-maneuvering his opponents.

This essay looks at Mathias' fight to fix the Bay, while the next one recounts the struggle for a memorial to honor Vietnam vets. Together they were among the most remarkable and lasting accomplishments of

Mathias' legislative career. In both cases, Mathias began the crusade alone in the Senate.

One of the people Mathias listened to most closely during his trip around the Bay in 1973 was waterman Larry Simns, who spoke not just for himself but for the many fishermen who were members of the Maryland Watermen's Association he led. He told Mathias that the fish were dying and that his catch had been way down for many years. He'd tried repeatedly to bring attention to the problem, but he wasn't being taken seriously. Experts told him anecdotes weren't enough, that he needed hard evidence—scientific data—to back up his claims. For Mathias, this was proof that there had to be a rigorous, formal study to document and explain the Bay's decline.[3]

Mathias took what he learned from the trip to President Nixon's EPA administrator, Russell Train, and enlisted Train's support for a serious examination that would lay out the problems and outline solutions. Train, a conservative but a staunch environmentalist, who later became head of the World Wildlife Fund, was receptive. Mathias and Train got experts to flesh out the details. Then Mathias had to get Congress to direct the EPA to conduct the study.

Mathias understood the politics would be difficult, since they always were with environmental issues, and because a study like this had never been done for any estuary anywhere in the country. But as a key member of the Senate Appropriations Committee and the leading Republican on the Appropriations subcommittee that funded the EPA, he managed to secure $27 million in total, with installments starting in 1976, for a multi-year study. Of course, he couldn't get this kind of funding alone. Among others, Maryland senator Paul Sarbanes and Maryland representatives Roy Dyson and Steny Hoyer, who always kept an eye out for what would help the entire state, helped push the money through.

Nothing happened quickly. It wasn't until September 1983, more than 10 years and several EPA administrators after the boat trip, that the study was finally ready. As a part of its charge, the EPA was to recommend a blueprint for action, and the agency would be key, directing the effort, pulling resources together, and marshalling federal, state and local governments, the scientific community, universities and advocacy groups.

The Bay watershed was not just one state; it spanned all or parts of six—Maryland, Virginia, Delaware, West Virginia, Pennsylvania, and New York, plus the District of Columbia—so the effort to fix it needed a leader for all of them. In a video shot on a boat in the Bay, Mathias aptly described this from the point of view of the creatures he had imagined so vividly as a boy. "There is no such thing as a 'part of the Bay,'" he said with the water stretching behind him. "What happens in every part of the Bay affects every other part ... the fish, the crabs and the oysters, they treat the Bay as a *unit*.... They move around....They are not impressed by the county lines and other artificial jurisdictional lines which make the Bay problems so difficult."[4]

Yes, but fish weren't politicians. One state wasn't going to tell the other states what to do. The EPA had to coordinate the effort, using the study recommendations to propose policies and regulations and to find the resources to make it all happen.

By the spring of 1983, as luck would have it, a new president—Reagan—had appointed a new head of the EPA, William Ruckelshaus. He replaced the wildly controversial administrator Anne Gorsuch, who'd been a political disaster, slashing the EPA budget, populating key positions with representatives of the very industries the agency regulated and so antagonizing both parties in Congress that she became a liability for the Reagan administration and was pushed out after less than two years.

By contrast, Ruckelshaus had a good reputation among environmentalists. He'd been the first EPA administrator, appointed to head the new agency by President Nixon. His record demonstrated that he was inclined to take seriously the agency's role as environmental steward. But he was now working for a conservative Republican president, Ronald Reagan, who seemed to adhere to the conservative, anti-regulation and pro-business orthodoxy on environmental protection. Foreseeing the battles over the Bay ahead, we needed Ruckelshaus not just to support the vital money, policy and programmatic measures but also to be an aggressive advocate.

Mathias' boat trip back in 1973 had been eye-opening for him, and he reasoned that the same experience might help Ruckelshaus understand first-hand how grim things were. So in July 1983, Mathias invited him on a one-day boat trip across the Bay and back, and Ruckelshaus accepted. Governor Harry Hughes made the Maryland state yacht *Aurora* available, and Hughes and his staff put together a tour designed to show how badly the Bay had declined. Hughes, who was the chief advocate and leader among governors, was crucial in the restoration effort.

Once the Bay state leaders got Ruckelshaus on the boat, they had a captive audience for the obvious degradation that had only gotten worse since Mathias' first boat trip 10 years earlier.

Mathias also needed to demonstrate to Ruckelshaus that there was broad, bipartisan political support for fixing the problem, so the boat was well stocked with top Republicans. Besides Mathias, there were Pennsylvania lieutenant governor William Scranton III and Virginia senator John Warner. Pennsylvania senator Arlen Specter came to the dock for the sendoff before the trip, and another Republican senator, Pennsylvania's John Heinz, who wasn't there, came to be very helpful. Key Democrats included, in addition to Governor Hughes, Virginia governor Chuck Robb and Mathias' Maryland colleague, Senator Paul Sarbanes—a native of the Eastern Shore.

Ruckelshaus was already inclined to want to help clean up the Bay. Now he became a passionate advocate.

In September 1983, the long-awaited Chesapeake Bay study was finally released. As we'd expected, it was very bad news, sounding the alarm that the Bay was dying. And there was a new culprit, not just "point source" pollution, such as industrial waste from individual industrial plants, but more diffuse and widespread "non-point" contaminants, such as agricultural and urban runoff, which Mathias had seen during his boat trip 10 years earlier.

Despite the grim message, there was hope because we were able to catalogue the causes of the decline in the Bay's water quality and living resources. And for the first time, we had targets, priorities and a plan of attack for reversing the problems.

Newspaper and TV coverage was an important part of the effort. When the Bay study was about to be released, we arranged a press conference for

A tour of the Chesapeake Bay conducted by Senator Mathias and Governor Harry Hughes (D–MD), 1983. Shown from left are Senator John Warner (R–VA); Governor Hughes; Lieutenant Governor William Scranton (R–PA); Senator Paul S. Sarbanes (D–MD); Governor Chuck Robb (D–VA); Senator Charles McC. Mathias, Jr. (R–MD); and William Ruckelshaus, EPA Administrator in the Reagan administration (Maryland Governor's Office photo).

Senator Mathias and EPA officials. Mathias was expecting an important but lower-level EPA official, such as the agency's director for the region that included the Bay. And he wasn't anticipating much publicity—reports like this one typically wind up collecting dust.

"So, who's coming?" he asked as we walked down the hall to the press conference. Ruckelshaus, I told him. He looked surprised. "Really?" he said.

It was unusual for the head of an agency to come to a press event like this, particularly when we were expecting bad news. It turned out this was a last-minute decision by Ruckelshaus, who could easily have delegated it to an underling. Mathias got to the room where the press conference was being held and opened the door. There must have been more than a dozen TV cameras, plus numerous print reporters, local and national. This was clearly going to be a much bigger story than we'd thought.

The EPA head would clearly be put on the spot. The first question was something along the lines of "OK, we see the Bay is dying, so what are you going to do about it?" Ruckelshaus said he was committed to getting the money, $4 million annually for EPA, and policies in place to launch the cleanup program. The resulting press attention was like rocket fuel for the cleanup effort.[5]

Having Ruckelshaus' support was a good start, but just a start. We needed money in the 1984 budget the Reagan administration was putting together in the winter of 1983. The problem was that the head of the Office of Management and Budget, David Stockman, was "Dr. No." He wanted zero money for the Bay. Stockman outranked Ruckelshaus: Agency heads had to submit their budgets to OMB officials, and OMB was the final arbiter.

Word leaked out before the budget was finalized (maybe through Ruckelshaus) that the Reagan administration wasn't including any money for the Bay. Without federal money and EPA leadership, the federal-state partnership simply wouldn't happen. But Ruckelshaus was a battle-tested infighter. In 1973, as deputy attorney general, he'd been a key player in the infamous Saturday Night massacre. Then, he showed his mettle by resigning instead of obeying President Nixon's order to fire Watergate special prosecutor Archibald Cox, who was investigating official misconduct by Nixon and his aides.

Mathias worked behind the scenes with Ruckelshaus, as I did with EPA staff, to try to get the Reagan White House to overturn Stockman's decision. We had help. Unlike today, most state and local newspapers had beat reporters covering their Congressional delegations, and they were writing stories that noted that while the Bay was dying, the Reagan administration was turning its back on the nation's largest estuary, right in Reagan's back yard. Reagan and his top staff were seeing this sort of negative coverage every day, in addition to similar stories on TV and in national newspapers.

Showing that the watershed states were all in was critical to our strategy. A strategic conference was held in December 1983, with Ruckelshaus, the governors of the three states that bordered on the Bay, and the mayor of the District of Columbia, among many others. This was the beginning of a coordinated and visible effort to restore the Bay. Tom Horton, a leading environmental writer who had explored every river in the Bay watershed, aptly characterized its significance. "This important conference really didn't do anything material for the Bay at first, but it put its plight on the map and implanted it in people's consciousness in a manner that wasn't going away," he said.[6]

Reagan already had an awful reputation on the environment. Not only had departed EPA administrator Anne Gorsuch set a terrible tone, but hardline Interior Secretary James Watt was even more controversial. Among other things, Republicans worried Watt's decision to back offshore drilling in California waters threatened GOP chances in Reagan's home state.

The White House desperately needed a success story—and we got one. Not only was Stockman ordered to reverse his decision on the Bay money, but we also got more than we were expecting—a $10 million annual commitment for four years. It sounds like peanuts now, but it's three times as much—$30 million a year—in 2023 dollars. Beyond that, the White House decided to single out Reagan's commitment to the Bay in his 1984 State of the Union speech, calling the Bay a national treasure.

This was huge. Being mentioned in the State of the Union address is priceless. It attracts media attention not just locally but nationally. The press coverage in turn makes it an invaluable platform for educating ordinary citizens who might have been unaware of the problem. There would be an uptick in interest and in donations flowing into campaigns to advocate for the cleanup, to non-profits and others engaged in the effort.

Reagan even made a visit to Tilghman Island, speaking to a largely Republican crowd of watermen in a closed firehouse, in an effort to "green up" as he ran for a second term.

During the next several years, Mathias continued to work to make sure federal money kept flowing into the Bay restoration effort. Not only that, but he also increased the number of federal agencies involved by bringing in the Fish and Wildlife Service, the National Oceanic and Atmospheric Administration, the Soil Conservation Service and the Army Corps of Engineers, among others.[7]

* * *

Mathias kept up his fight to restore the Chesapeake Bay until he retired in early 1987. Later that year he gave the keynote speech for one of the most pivotal events in the Bay cleanup effort. The administrator of the

EPA, the governors of Bay watershed states and the mayor of the District of Columbia had all come together for the signing of the Chesapeake Bay Agreement. For the first time, the EPA and states surrounding the Bay set explicit goals for reducing pollution, agreed to deadlines to restore the Bay and committed the resources to do it.

This was a major first step, but it should be noted that Mathias wanted something even stronger. Mathias had sought a Bay agreement with more teeth than the one he got. This would have saved a lot of time, as the largely voluntary program finally had to be made more regulatory, but not until 2010.

I was lucky to be with him that day in 1987. I could see the glow on his face. How satisfying it must have been to witness 15 years of work start to pay off. What he had envisioned back in 1973, when the *Miss Afton IV* left the dock in Baltimore to carry him around the Bay, was finally happening.

Today the federal-state-local infrastructure that began back then has survived and grown even stronger, thanks to the continuing partnership between the Bay states and the federal government, plus the work of other senators, members of the U.S. House, governors and state legislators, scientists, local officials and local communities that followed what Mathias began.

This special EPA program for the Bay remains the only one in the nation for an estuary. Officials throughout the watershed are united toward restoring the Bay, but it hasn't been easy, and progress has been slow. On the one hand, the Bay is inarguably cleaner and healthier than it would have been without the effort Mathias began so many years ago. On the other hand, there are frequent reminders that success is far from automatic.

In 2011, a dead zone, where oysters, fish and other marine life were dying in oxygen-starved water, stretched an astonishing 83 miles, from Baltimore Harbor south to where the Potomac River empties into the estuary. But in 2018, while giving the Bay's health just an overall grade of C, the University of Maryland Center for Environmental Science found that for the first time in 33 years, the Bay had demonstrated improvement in every region, a sign the cleanup effort was working. Bottle-nosed dolphins were spotted playing in the Bay near Cambridge, Maryland, and in a sign sobering for swimmers but good news for environmentalists, scientists hooked two great white sharks in the Bay's Virginia waters.

Environmental writer Horton sums up the state of the Bay today. "By 2021, it was clear that the Bay restoration program had wrung remarkable cleanup progress from sewage treatment and from controls on air pollution—dirty air contributes nearly a third of nitrogen, the Bay's largest pollutant," Horton said. "But meeting cleanup goals will require major progress in other areas as well, from controlling agricultural runoff, still exempt from many clean water laws, and from controlling development, even as a million or more new people move to the watershed every decade."

Mathias knew the work was only beginning. In the future, he said, when he spoke in 1987 at the signing of the Chesapeake Bay Agreement, this would "be reckoned as one of the truly significant days in the history of man and the Bay. ... There are many visions of history, but all of them must include the job of a laborer who sees his work continue after he has left the vineyard."

NOTES

1. Michael Fincham, "Chesapeake Crossing, the Voyages of Mac Mathias," *Chesapeake Quarterly* 14, https://www.chesapeakequarterly.net/V14N2/.

2. Mathias keynote speech at 1987 Chesapeake Bay conference.

3. Larry Simns remarks (reflections) at Mathias retirement celebration, August 1986.

4. Chesapeake Bay Commission 40th anniversary, video, 2020, https://www.chesbay. U.S.

5. Ben Franklin, "Chesapeake Study Citing Pollution Threats," *The New York Times*, September 27, 1983, https://www.nytimes.com/1983/09/27/U.S./chesapeake-bay-study-citing-pollution-threats.html

6. Chesapeake Bay Agreements, December 1983 conference, EPA.gov.

7. U.S. Senate Subcommittee on Government Efficiency and the District of Columbia, "Future of the Chesapeake Bay Program," December 1986, p. 3.

Healing the Wounds of Vietnam

Monica Healy

The dedication of the Vietnam Veterans Memorial took place on a cold and rainy November 13, 1982, following several days of events to honor Vietnam vets.

At the dedication, we watched grown men break down and weep as they found on the Wall the names of their friends who'd died years before, thousands of miles away. This memorial meant the world to them and, as it turned out, to people who'd never been to Vietnam and to people who'd been on opposite sides of the bitter debate over the war. It's difficult to go to the Wall and not be moved.

This also was a proud and emotional day for the senior senator from Maryland, Charles "Mac" Mathias. What he had envisioned when he first agreed to take the lead in the Senate to establish a Vietnam Veterans Memorial had finally become real.

Despite its rocky beginning, the Vietnam Veterans Memorial has been an unqualified success. The Wall has fulfilled the purpose its creators intended—to bring together those who were for and against the war and to begin to heal the nation's wounds from the war. At the beginning, though, it was hard to imagine that would ever happen. Instead, the struggle to create the Memorial reopened all those wounds.

The effort dates back to 1979. Jan Scruggs and his colleague Bob Doubek, both Vietnam vets themselves, were pushing the idea to build a Memorial for those who fought and those who died in Vietnam.

The two met with Senator Mathias in early August of that year. They wanted him to be their congressional champion, to lead the legislative effort to authorize the Memorial. I was there at the first meeting. Jan Scruggs, Bob Doubek and the third member of the trio, Jack Wheeler, also a vet, who was not at the meeting, were just a ragtag group, but they had a great idea. They had raised very little money (the Memorial was to be privately funded) and had only recently incorporated, creating the Vietnam

Vietnam Veterans Memorial Wall. Visitors in front of the wall on Memorial Day weekend, May 24, 2008 (AP Photo/J. David Ake).

Veterans Memorial Fund (VVMF). They had no plan, no strategy. In fact, the reason Jan Scruggs picked Senator Mathias was not strategic but because Mathias happened to be one of his two senators. Scruggs was from Bowie, Maryland.

Scruggs had conceived of the idea of a Vietnam memorial after seeing the movie *The Deer Hunter*, a much-honored film about how the war changed the lives of a group of working men from Pennsylvania. He was distraught over the way Vietnam veterans had been treated when they came home.

I was new to the issue, and I didn't know how Mathias was going to react. Mathias went with his instincts—he just seemed to have a sixth sense. Without reservation, in that very first meeting, he said, "I'll do it, I'll take the lead." Scruggs and Doubek were surprised, since at most they'd expected a noncommittal "I'll get back to you." Me, too.

He was placing a lot of trust in the trio. One of his senior staffers advised Mathias before the meeting not to take a role. It was too risky, he said; not enough time had elapsed since the end of the war and the country was certainly not ready to heal.

In the meeting, though, Mathias agreed that he felt badly about how Vietnam vets were treated after the war. Going against his own party, Mathias had been an early advocate of withdrawing troops from Vietnam. In fact, he called for the withdrawal of troops when he first ran for the

Senate in 1968. He had served in Japan during World War II and had seen first-hand war's awful toll. That experience, according to his son Charles, helped form his instinctive caution about committing the United States to war.

The theme of the memorial effort was to heal the nation, to bring together those who'd been opposed to the war and those who'd been for it by honoring all who had served and especially those who'd died. Mathias thought the memorial could go a long way toward healing the divisions. He asked me to be the lead staffer.

As it turned out, Mathias' instincts about the ability of the group to deliver proved to be on target. The VVMF team all had different strengths, and they complemented each other. The son of a milkman, Scruggs was an infantryman who had pulled himself up by his bootstraps. He usually wore blue jeans, and he became the face of the movement. He was relentless and a force of nature. Doubek, a lawyer by trade, was great at organization, messaging and details. Wheeler, a West Point grad and Yale lawyer, was the visionary and strategist. They turned out to be an unusually effective team.

To succeed in this legislative effort, Mathias knew he had to seek out someone who supported the war as the lead co-sponsor. It's common in Congress to recruit someone from the other side of the aisle to demonstrate bipartisanship, but in this case, it also meant reaching out to a hawk on the war—and very few Democrats had been that. He asked Virginia Republican Senator John Warner to be a chief co-sponsor. Warner immediately said yes. It seemed like a clairvoyant choice. As it turned out, our main opposition was to come from the right, the hawks. Warner had been the secretary of the Navy during Vietnam. He signed orders sending thousands of Marines and sailors into combat, and it weighed heavily on his conscience that many did not come home.

Mathias, while a Republican, had a more liberal voting record than many Democrats. The Democrats were in the majority during that period and felt comfortable with Mathias. Like him, most of them had opposed the war.

Warner turned out to be the perfect co-sponsor. He served as liaison with many of the conservative, more hawkish Republicans in the Senate, and he could comfortably take the lead when we later had to deal with controversial Secretary of the Interior James Watt, who threw endless roadblocks in the way. Warner always looked at himself as a foot soldier, perhaps because of his military background and the fact that he was technically junior to Mathias in the Senate. But he took a leadership role in raising private money for the memorial. In this Warner had a powerful secret weapon in his wife Elizabeth Taylor, who was catnip for fundraisers.

Mathias always thought of Warner as indispensable because he played so many roles.

Before they rolled out the legislation, the two senators knew it was important to inoculate themselves against the criticism they knew they'd get from the right and the left, from the hawks and the doves. So they convinced former presidential nominees on opposite sides of the war to co-sponsor the bill. Senator Barry Goldwater (R–AZ), who ran for the presidency in 1964, was the hawk, and Senator George McGovern (D–ND), an anti-war candidate for the presidency in 1972, was the dove. The two were able to come together on this important issue, and the bill was introduced right before Veterans Day, on November 8, 1979.

Mathias and Warner personally pushed the issue on a regular basis, reaching out to their colleagues to get them to sign on as co-sponsors, holding press conferences and chairing meetings to advance the cause. At the same time, the senators and their staffs deployed Scruggs and his colleagues plus volunteers to lobby the old-fashioned way, door to door, Senate office to Senate office, to try to line up more co-sponsors.

We were also fortunate to have a lot of well-connected people from inside and outside Congress lining up support. Stan Kimmitt, the secretary of the Senate appointed by the Senate majority leader Robert Byrd (D–WV), had the clout that came with his role in the leadership. He had a son who'd gone to Vietnam. He worked behind the scenes and recruited several co-sponsors. Max Cleland, a triple amputee who'd lost parts of two legs and an arm in Vietnam and served as the administrator of the Veterans Administration under Jimmy Carter, was also a fierce advocate.

This all paid off.

It's very unusual for any bill to move quickly. And for the rare ones that do become law, it usually takes years of hard work. But the Vietnam Veterans Memorial legislation came to the Senate floor in record time, on April 30, 1980, less than six months from the time it was introduced. Every member of the Senate co-sponsored the bill. I remember being on the floor that day when Senate minority leader Howard Baker (R–TN) turned to Mathias and asked, "Am I a co-sponsor?" Mathias assured him he was. This was too important to be the lone person out. Even majority leader Byrd departed from the tradition of majority leaders not co-sponsoring legislation and signed on.

After the Senate passed it, though, we still had to get it through the House. Representative John Paul Hammerschmidt (R–AR) (whose claim to fame was beating Bill Clinton for a congressional seat in 1974), the ranking member on the House Veterans Committee, took the lead to move the bill through the House. It didn't go smoothly. Liberal Representative Phillip Burton (D-CA), who was in charge of a major subcommittee that had

Mathias, Vietnam veterans and staff members. Senator Mathias is fifth from left, and immediately to his left are Jack Wheeler, Monica Healy, Jan Scruggs and Bob Doubek (U.S. Senate photographer).

jurisdiction over the National Park Service, was territorial and protective of the National Mall, which he considered his turf. Plus, he'd opposed the war and saw this as a pro-war effort.

Nor did he like the fact that the Senate legislation specified the site where the memorial would be built. Picking a site was always left to the National Park Service. In this case, though, Mathias had personally picked the site, Constitution Gardens, near the Lincoln Memorial. He picked the Mall because it had been a battleground of opinion and dissent during the war. He said that he "felt the proximity to the Lincoln Memorial was fitting because not since the Civil War had the nation suffered wounds and divisions as those endured over Vietnam."

Burton's opposition was potentially a major problem, and because of that, the House-passed bill did not list a specific site. But after ferocious lobbying by the VVMF trio and others, Burton succumbed, and we prevailed in the conference negotiations between the House and the Senate. The final bill included the site Mathias had picked.

President Jimmy Carter signed the measure into law on July 1, 1980, in a White House Rose Garden ceremony. It was a wonderful moment, but in retrospect we were way too confident at that point, with no idea what was about to hit us.

After the legislation became law, the next step was to pick a design. The design competition was the largest ever held in the United States. Prominent architects and sculptors were on the jury. It was 1981, and by then Ronald Reagan was president. An Asian American Yale undergraduate, Maya Lin, won the competition. Her design was a landscape solution—two intersecting, polished granite walls backed into the earth in the shape of a V.

Most of the veterans involved in the effort saw the design as dignified. However, a small but very powerful group thought it resembled a ditch or a gravestone—an implicit condemnation of the war. Ross Perot, an early supporter of the memorial and major funder of the design competition, denounced it as an insult to veterans. Perot, an aggressive, outspoken business tycoon who later ran for president as an independent against George H.W. Bush and Bill Clinton, led the fight against the design. Similar strong opposition came from Jim Webb, a Vietnam vet and an early proponent of the memorial who'd been helpful on the staff of the House Veterans Affairs Committee in moving the legislation through the House. He was a well-known author and later became the secretary of the navy and a U.S. senator from Virginia.

The point of Maya Lin's design was to make a neutral statement, reflecting the theme of reconciliation. But opponents thought it was anything but neutral—they derided the V-shaped memorial set into the ground as "a black gash of shame."

So began a well-organized effort to stop the memorial in its current design. In addition to Perot and Webb, opponents included powerful members of Congress, predominantly from the House: the conservative, outspoken and controversial Representative Henry Hyde (R–IL), Representative Donald Bailey, a conservative Democrat from Pennsylvania, and Rep. Duncan Hunter (R–CA), among others. The group used every tool they could, including Dear Colleague letters to fellow members, congressional resolutions, op-eds, letters to Secretary Watt, news stories—anything that might derail the effort. The fight became bitter.

It was clear the group intended to delay the project, alter the design or even kill the memorial if they couldn't change Maya Lin's design. Ominously, the fight reopened the wounds of the war itself. While the group of opponents was small, they were determined, well connected and powerful. They were also skillful at using conservative media to join the battle. Luckily, we had influential supporters on the right, such as James Kilpatrick, a well-known columnist. The opponents found a crucial ally in Interior Secretary Watt, who was in a key position to step in and stall the project, if not kill it altogether.

The fight soon became very high profile. Mainstream press including wire services, *The Washington Post*, *The New York Times*, *The Wall Street Journal*, *The Baltimore Sun*, plus other regional papers around the country, TV news and shows such as *60 Minutes* all covered the story. Major veterans' groups were engaged in the effort, almost all in support of the design. Ordinary Americans got involved. Even celebrities such as Bob Hope lent their names to the memorial effort.

Mathias, Warner, and their allies knew that they had a serious problem, since a nasty, protracted fight would only hurt the memorial, even if proponents of the design ultimately won. It was clear that some way had to be found to placate the opponents.

Warner organized a meeting with the side Mathias called the "militarists," led by Perot, to try to work out a compromise. Each side agreed to send the same number of negotiators, but Perot and his team ignored the rules, and their side far outnumbered the proponents.

A heated, emotional, five-hour meeting took place in late January 1982 in the Senate Armed Services Committee room. Jan Scruggs was on the verge of tears. Mathias didn't show up and I'm not sure why since he never said. I like to give him the benefit of the doubt, that his staying away was strategic, as he may have thought he was not the right person to be in the room forging a compromise with the militarists. Senator Warner was the right person to take the lead.

Indeed, Warner captured the intensity of the moment later in a speech. He recalled at one point during the meeting that Brigadier General George Price "had stood up, tall and strong, and shouted: 'If I hear another dissent, I'm going to grab him by the scruff and throw him out of the room!'"

Finally, a compromise was forged, suggested by another general, Michael Davison, who had served in Vietnam and helped lead the invasion of Cambodia. He suggested adding a heroic statue of three fighting men and flag. A deal was struck, setting the stage for the groundbreaking.

Even though the group at the Warner meeting worked out this compromise, it wasn't good enough for Secretary Watt, who kept adding other demands.

There was growing frustration over Watt's obstinance. By then the interior secretary was very controversial, a lightning rod for the Reagan administration. A hardline conservative, he was the official who wouldn't allow the Beach Boys to play on the Mall on the Fourth of July.

Mathias, Warner, and team VVMF pushed the White House hard to get Watt to back off. They sent letters, made phone calls, and appealed personally to White House staff. Chief of Staff James Baker and his deputy, Mike Deaver, a communications guru, were keeping an eye on it. We were told they did not like being put in the middle of the fight and preferred to stay out of it.

Two months later, after relentless pressure on the White House, Watt backed off and approved the permit. The groundbreaking took place in March 1982.

But the fight was hardly over. Even though Watt had approved the permit that allowed the project to go forward, another controversy had arisen over the placement of the statue and flags. That dogged us throughout the year, and Watt's obstinance threatened but in the end failed to stop the dedication of the memorial two days after Veterans Day in 1982 and the celebration activities around it.

This was still not the end of the fight. Representatives Bailey, Hunter and Hyde were able to get a House resolution passed placing the flag above the apex of the memorial's V-shaped walls with the statue in front of it, something Watt supported. Mathias blocked the legislation in the Senate. It was the job of the Fine Arts Commission to pick the location of the flag and the statue, not Congress, and to integrate all three elements in a way that would symbolically reconcile the nation's bitter ambivalence about the war without compromising the artistic integrity of the design.

To try to resolve this issue, Mathias asked Secretary Watt to meet with him and Warner in January 1983, two months after the memorial dedication. They wanted to convince him to leave the decision in the hands of the Fine Arts Commission, where it belonged. Watt pushed back belligerently, at one point telling the senators he thought the design was "an act of treason."

As Senator Mathias' staff member on the matter, I took copious notes. I couldn't believe my ears. I dutifully wrote down Watt's phrase. After the meeting, Philip Geyelin, a good friend and columnist for *The Washington Post*, called to ask about the meeting. Somewhat naively I gave him the details, including Watt's incendiary remark. Memo to self: Even longtime journalist friends are reporters first unless you specify ahead of time that your comments are off the record—something I should have learned long ago, since my father was a White House reporter.

Shortly afterward, Geyelin's column appeared, which focused on the latest turn in Watt's obstructionist tactics. Geyelin had been head of the *Post*'s editorial board during the Vietnam War and had used his persuasive powers to turn the *Post*'s editorial position against the war. Washington insiders respected him and regularly read his columns.[1]

Geyelin mentioned Watt's "act of treason" comment. The column didn't specifically say when Watt had said it, carefully disguising the meeting. But someone had leaked it. I had to own up to Mathias that I was that someone, so I dutifully walked into his office and fessed up. He gave me his familiar poker face look. I had no idea what he was thinking. Was he furious? Was I about to be fired? Or did he like the fact I leaked the comment as a way to use the media to apply pressure on the White House to get Watt to back off? I never knew what he was thinking. He never told me.

It got worse. The Interior Department flatly denied that Watt ever said that. But I doubled-checked my notes and confirmed its accuracy to Geyelin. The *Post* stood by the column, and Interior officials reluctantly acknowledged the truth.

Later that month, Watt made yet another costly mistake. Speaking at a chamber of commerce meeting, he said it was fine with him if the fight over the statute and the flag lingered indefinitely, for several years. This was reported in *The Washington Post*, and at that point, Baker, Deaver and senior counselor Ed Meese—even Reagan himself, we were told—had had enough. They didn't want an endless rehashing of the Vietnam War to be a distraction. They had far more pressing international issues to focus on. They ordered Watt to back off, paving the way for the permit approval soon thereafter.[2]

It's impossible to know whether Mathias' instant decision at that first meeting with Jan Scruggs and Bob Doubek was the key to making the memorial happen. Maybe the Wall would eventually have come about somehow without him (though perhaps not at his handpicked site). But Mathias was uniquely qualified to help make it happen. He had the insight to see how important it could be, the conviction and nerve to take it on, and the credibility to bring it to life, even when he was getting all kinds of advice to stay away. His leadership, support, and ability to attract allies gave the cause instant credibility, something Scruggs, Doubek and Wheeler desperately needed. He also worked almost obsessively to get the bill passed and the memorial built, going head to head with opponents, mostly from his own party, who tried to thwart the effort and derail the project.

Mathias would continue to honor Vietnam veterans and be involved in memorial activities for the rest of his life. In 2007, he was invited to speak at the 25th anniversary of the dedication of the memorial. His health was not good, and I didn't think he would show up. He was frail and had difficulty walking. But he was determined to celebrate the memorial's impact and success, and his poor health wasn't going to stand in the way. He had the courage to come.

When it was time for him to speak, he stood up shakily. It was touching to see his former wingman, John Warner, come to his side and help him get to the podium. Mathias addressed Jan Scruggs, who stood on the stage next to him. "Jan, I remember when we talked about reconciliation. Today, it's a reality … with the passage of time, we have seen the importance of the Wall increase, and it will continue to increase as history goes down its long path. Vietnam veterans are recognized and acknowledged and appreciated as never before."

"So I salute Jan and his colleagues as they guard the Wall."[3]

NOTES

1. Philip Geyelin, "The Vietnam Memorial (Con't)," *The Washington Post*, January 11, 1983, https://www.washingtonpost.com/archive/politics/1983/01/11/the-vietnam-memorial-contd/7abb21f7-01f1-40c1-ad7f-d25be44f92d9/.

2. Phil McCombs, "Watt Stalls Addition to Vietnam Memorial," *The Washington Post*, January 29, 1983, https://www.washingtonpost.com/archive/lifestyle/1983/01/29/watt-stalls-addition-to-vietnam-memorial/8b96034a-2d22-438e-90a2-1160972740fb/.

3. CSPAN, 25th anniversary of the Vietnam Memorial, March 26, 2007, https://www.c-span.org/video/?197330-1/25th-anniversary-vietnam-veterans-memorial.

An Impressive Legacy
in Foreign Affairs

CASIMIR YOST

In the spring of 1977, Senator Charles Mathias was appointed as a Senate advisor to the Strategic Arms Limitation Talks (SALT) being conducted between U.S. and Soviet negotiators in Geneva. He took this assignment seriously and in July traveled to Geneva and met with negotiators from both sides.

He was particularly effective in pointing out to the Soviets the challenges to achieving a two-thirds vote in the U.S. Senate in favor of a SALT treaty and underlining the importance of credible and effective verification measures in the emerging treaty. He did so with a quintessential Mathias touch. Talking to senior Soviet negotiators, he described how as a boy he would watch his mother buy strawberries from a street vendor in his hometown of Frederick, Maryland. She would, according to Mathias, examine the strawberries at the bottom of the bucket to ensure that they were as fresh as those at the top. The Soviet officials delighted in the story and got its point.

I worked for Senator Mathias for the better part of a decade beginning in 1977—first on the senator's personal staff and then on the staff of the Senate Foreign Relations Committee, which the senator joined in 1981. I traveled with him regularly to Europe, Latin America, the Soviet Union and the Middle East and I had the opportunity to observe him first-hand for the better part of a decade. It was a pleasure and an honor. I was never embarrassed by a Mathias question or comment. He was frequently the smartest person in the room, though he hid this fact by explaining that he was just a "poor country lawyer."

He was a veteran of the U.S. Navy in World War II, and Senator Mathias' views on war and arms control were profoundly affected by visits to Hiroshima and Nagasaki shortly after the end of the war. He would say, in describing these visits, "I have seen what a relatively small nuclear device can do to a city." He had a special affinity for other members of Congress who had served in the war; more than 100 members of the Senate had done so.

Mathias was an early opponent of the Vietnam War and retained in his papers a copy of the Tonkin Gulf Resolution personally signed by President Lyndon Johnson. It is likely that he regretted his vote as a member of the House of Representatives for that resolution, as did many of his colleagues. As a first-term senator, he led efforts to repeal the resolution. He opposed efforts by President Nixon to expand U.S. military operations into Laos and Cambodia. He supported the War Powers Resolution of 1973, which sought to limit presidential power to commit U.S. troops to combat without congressional authority. He was a member in 1975 of the so-called Church Committee, formed to investigate abuses by the CIA and other U.S. government agencies. He subsequently served on the U.S. Senate Select Committee on Intelligence and other committees with international jurisdiction, including the Appropriations Committee Foreign Operations Subcommittee and the Foreign Relations Committee.

Mathias supported an expanded role for Congress in the making of foreign policy after the Vietnam War and in examining the abuses of power perpetuated by successive administrations. But he was also candid about the drawbacks of having so many legislative cooks in the foreign policy kitchen.

* * *

His interests focused on the Soviet Union and arms control, Europe and alliance relations, the Middle East and, later in his career, trade and energy issues.

Mathias was intensely curious and not afraid of risks. Once he hopped a ride on a U.S. Navy P3, anti-submarine, maritime surveillance aircraft, which was going on routine patrol between the naval air station on the Patuxent River in Maryland and Iceland. He took me along for the ride. He also welcomed a chance to fly in the co-pilot seat of a new navy jet to see how it landed on an aircraft carrier. He frequently took side trips from his official itinerary when traveling abroad.

He was equally at ease with presidents and Soviet World War II veterans. He was—to the occasional frustration of his domestic staffers—an inveterate traveler. He brought historical context to his travels; Samuel Johnson and Edmund Burke were his constant companions. His depth and breadth of knowledge was impressive to his foreign interlocutors, who were more accustomed to Americans who lived in the moment.

He was also a moderate Northeast Republican in a party that was drifting—some would say galloping—right and South. His philosophically compatible Senate friends on issues of foreign policy—John Sherman Cooper, Clifford Case, Jacob Javits, Edward Brooke, Charles Percy—were not in tune with the evolving direction of the party. Mathias' instinct was to moderate, to soften edges. Jesse Helms and his ilk were not into moderation and softening. Ronald Reagan took the party in a new direction, leaving Mathias and company to grasp for relevance.

* * *

My association with Senator Mathias was an unlikely match in many respects. I had spent the previous five years working as a banker in the Middle East and South Asia. I had never worked on Capitol Hill and had little prior experience with some of the senator's core interests such as arms control. I did have good academic credentials and came from a well-traveled Foreign Service family.

I initially spent an hour or so in the spring of 1977 with Senator Mathias in his Capitol "hideaway" office—a seniority perk. He asked neither my party registration nor whether I was from Maryland. We did discuss the Middle East at some length. A few days later, I was offered the job as his defense and foreign policy staffer and I accepted it. In retrospect, I suspect the senator used the interview to gauge whether he would enjoy spending extended periods on Pan American flights with me. I am grateful he took the risk.

The early weeks in his office were eventful. The Carter administration had recently taken office, and Mathias was viewed as an essential Republican vote on issues ranging from the Panama Canal treaties to a possible Strategic Arms Limitation Treaty to arms sales to Arab countries. Years later the senator was to observe that President Carter and President Reagan, for that matter, were both hampered by not appreciating the reach and complexity of the U.S. government.[1]

He was not impressed by Carter's symbolic cost-cutting measures such as selling the presidential yacht, the *Sequoia*, which presidents dating back to the 1920s had used to entertain and solicit support from members of Congress and others. When a senior Carter administration official asked Mathias how Carter's poor relations with Washington's elite could be repaired, Mathias said, simply, "Buy back the *Sequoia*." This said, President Carter always treated Senator Mathias with great courtesy—better by far than the treatment he received from the Reagan administration. I sat in on two meetings on foreign relations topics in the Oval Office with President Carter, and both times the president was attentive to what Mathias had to say.

Within weeks of joining the senator's staff I departed with him on a trip that took us to Geneva, Paris, London and Belgium. As noted above, Mathias had been appointed as a Senate advisor to the Strategic Arms

President Carter and Mathias at the White House, September 22, 1978 (Mathias Family).

Limitation Talks (SALT) in Geneva. We were briefed by Ambassador Paul Warnke, the lead negotiator, and his staff and met with Soviet negotiators, and Mathias participated in two plenary negotiations on this trip.

The senator next traveled to France, Britain and Belgium to hear European and NATO perspectives on the proposed treaty. Mathias was all too familiar with the American practice of imposing finished decisions on our allies even when their interests were affected by those decisions. In his trip report to Senate colleagues, he wrote, "Many Western European governments feel they are getting unclear or contradictory signals from the Carter Administration."[2]

Mathias believed that part of his charge was to pressure the Carter administration to improve its consultations with allies. (In fairness to the administration, there was concern that one or more NATO member governments would have communist party coalition partners.)

* * *

After two weeks in Europe we returned to day-to-day Senate life. I was responsible for staffing the senator on the Foreign Operations Subcommittee of the Appropriations Committee. This subcommittee had jurisdiction over U.S. aid and assistance programs. The senator's simple instructions to me were "Take care of the Johns Hopkins University Bologna Center and the Asia Foundation." Both received U.S. government funding.

Directions from Senator Mathias were, like that brief charge, often sparse and lacking in detail. Mathias was not into micromanaging his staff. I know that this was a source of frustration to some staff members who wanted more guidance from the boss. I never felt that way in part because I traveled so much with him that I developed a good sense of where he would end up on a given issue, if not always the route that he would take to get there.

He was selective in taking positions on controversial issues. He was experienced enough to know that hot-button issues evolve over time and that premature judgment had its risks. Thus, he was publicly supportive of the SALT treaty as the negotiations proceeded. On the other hand, he was frustratingly uncommitted to supporting the Panama Canal treaties despite those treaties having been negotiated by Republican and Democratic presidents and enjoying bipartisan support. In the end he voted in favor, but he was hardly a leader in the ratification battle.

We also had to be attentive to Maryland-based defense industries, such as Fairchild Industries, with offices in Hagerstown, Maryland, that produced the A-10 ground support plane—an important "tank buster" asset in Middle East wars to come. I made an early mistake in not appreciating that the radar on the AWACS surveillance aircraft that the Carter administration considered selling to the shah of Iran was produced in a GE plant in Rep. Barbara Mikulski's district. I overstepped my writ in signing Mathias on to a "Dear Colleague" letter asking for a study of the sale with an opponent of the sale, Senator John Culver of Iowa. Representative Mikulski objected, but Mathias never criticized me for over-reaching. The shah was deposed before that sale went through.

The Carter and Reagan years were filled with challenging foreign policy issues requiring congressional review and concurrence. Senator Mathias was an important vote on these issues and was expected to have informed views on a wide range of complex national security matters.

During the Carter years, these included the Panama Canal treaties, arms sales to Arab nations in the Middle East, the issues that arose from the Camp David Arab-Israeli negotiations, the fall of the shah of Iran and the subsequent hostage crisis, the normalization of diplomatic relations with the Peoples Republic of China, and the Soviet invasion of Afghanistan. During the Reagan presidency, they included Israel's invasion of Lebanon, the Iran-Iraq war and the highly controversial deployment of

Pershing missiles in western Europe. Few issues, however, captured the senator's attention more than U.S.-Soviet relations.

* * *

The specter of Hiroshima and Nagasaki hung over how Senator Mathias viewed U.S. relations with the Soviet Union. He was keenly aware that the Cuban missile crisis was a near miss. He was never naïve about the risks to U.S. interests posed by the Soviets, but he believed that our mutual interests required that Moscow and Washington press ahead on arms control negotiations despite our deep differences on other issues.

The senator made four trips to the USSR in 1975, 1978, 1981 and 1985. I accompanied him on all but the first. On the 1978 trip, we went to the Soviet republics of Moldova and Ukraine and to the Central Asian cities of Tashkent, Bukhara and Samarkand in Uzbekistan. I was continually amazed at Mathias' ability to empathize with his Soviet hosts, while speaking frankly about the differences between our two countries. I remember a chance encounter in Central Asia between the senator and a grizzled Soviet veteran of World War II. The latter was clearly under the influence of too much vodka. Nonetheless, with the benefit of a translator, the two veterans reminisced at length about their wartime experiences.

On each of his visits to Moscow, Mathias was given broad access to Soviet military, diplomatic and intelligentsia leadership. He had extended one-on-one discussions with, among others, Foreign Minister Andrei Gromyko and Chief of the General Staff Marshall Nikolai Ogarkov. The senator noted in his report to the Senate, after his 1978 trip, that the Soviet leaders' "greatest concern was that some military relationship would develop between the Peoples Republic of China and the United States."[3]

On January 1, 1979, the United States and the PRC began formal diplomatic relations. There is some irony that 43 years later, American national security officials worry about the maturing military-to-military ties between the Russian Federation and the PRC.

The Soviet invasion of Afghanistan in 1979 and the ascension of Ronald Reagan to the U.S. presidency put arms control on the back burner for some years. On subsequent Mathias trips to Moscow, Russians looked to Mathias if not for reassurance then at least for explanation for the hardening of U.S. attitudes.

Mathias was to write during this period that "we [Americans] need to develop a far clearer understanding of the complexity of Soviet motivations." He went on to say, "We cannot zigzag crazily between the euphoria of détente and the paranoia engendered by the Soviet involvement in Africa and the Middle East."[4]

Arguably, these views have enduring relevance today as the United

States seeks to craft policies toward the People's Republic of China and the Russian Federation.

* * *

Senator Mathias was a welcome and regular visitor to London, Bonn and Paris. European leaders appreciated the opportunity to engage with a well-informed U.S. senator who did not insist on lecturing them on policy differences and genuinely tried to understand their perspectives on the issues of the day. One memorable trip involved visiting several French nuclear facilities as a guest of the French government. Then as now, France had a robust civilian nuclear energy generating program, and Mathias was convinced we needed to learn from French experiences.

He was a welcome interlocutor in Europe during the presidency of Jimmy Carter, whose mixed signals and homespun style did not always garner the Europeans' respect. During the early years of the Reagan presidency, Mathias had to do a good deal of hand holding with European friends, who were fearful of what the "cowboy president" might do.

Senator Mathias particularly enjoyed engaging with other Western, democratic parliamentarians. He believed that national legislatures truly pursued the people's business.

Among his proudest associations was with the North Atlantic Assembly (subsequently renamed the NATO Parliamentary Assembly). It provided a forum for parliamentarians from NATO member countries to meet and discuss challenges to the alliance. Senator Mathias chaired the Senate delegation to the Assembly and, in his final two years in office, assumed its presidency. Note for the record: Assembly deliberations were always conducted in attractive European settings with a consistently high quality of food and wine.

Senator Mathias' House counterpart was a long serving Democratic congressman from Texas, Jack Brooks, who had decided views and sharp elbows. Even so, he and Mathias got along well.

Mathias saw CODELS (official congressional delegations traveling abroad), such as those attending North Atlantic Assembly meetings, as offering important opportunities to present bipartisan images of the United States overseas. Moreover, he saw them as useful bonding experiences for members of Congress, allowing them to leave behind the partisan rancor at home. On one of his trips to Moscow, he and Democratic senator Alan Cranston of California teamed up. It was not a likely association, but it worked well because they shared similar views on arms control.

* * *

No region absorbed as much attention for Senator Mathias as the Middle East. Needless to say, he had a large number of constituents and supporters who were very interested in his views and votes on Middle East issues. Within weeks of joining his staff I was asked to give a foreign policy speech in the senator's stead at a Maryland synagogue—he was detained by back-to-back votes on the Senate floor. I found the audience was well disposed to Senator Mathias and believed him to be attentive to their concerns across a broad range of issues, domestic and foreign.

There is no question that the senator had upset those constituents who were focused primarily on his support for Israel. The American Israeli Public Affairs Committee, a lobby group that appeared to believe that U.S. Middle East interests were best defined in Jerusalem, did not consider Mathias a reliable vote.

The Baltimore Jewish Times carried an article titled "Mathias and Israel: Where Does He Stand?"[5] This article was written in reaction to a 1981 *Foreign Affairs* article by Mathias titled "Ethnic Groups and Foreign Policy." That article examined the historical evolution of political activism by ethnic lobbies in the United States and the outsized influence they brought to bear on American administrations. Not surprisingly, its treatment of Greek and Jewish lobbies attracted special attention, particularly in light of Senator Mathias' vote in support of a controversial arms sale to

Mathias shakes hands with President Sadat of Egypt, 1983 (photograph by Asfar Youssef).

Mathias and President Indira Gandhi, New Delhi, 1973 (Mathias Family).

Saudi Arabia in 1978. Critics of the senator also noted that he met in 1975 in Beirut with PLO chief Yasir Arafat well before it was acceptable to do so.

My own view remains that the Jewish community of Maryland appreciated his broad commitment to civil rights and issues of social justice. They applauded his eagerness to work for the release of Jewish "refuseniks" from the Soviet Union. Mathias had pressed Foreign Minister Gromyko on specific refusenik cases that had attracted his support and that of the Maryland Jewish community. They appreciated his willingness to listen carefully to their concerns. And perhaps they agreed with the arguments Mathias offered in the *Foreign Affairs* article that "the Soviet noose around the Middle East is tightening" and that Israel and Saudi Arabia shared this common enemy.[6]

He could not have anticipated that the U.S. military-to-military relationship with Saudi Arabia was an important factor in the successful response to Saddam Hussein's invasion of Kuwait in 1990. Nor, indeed, could he have anticipated the warming relations between the Gulf States and Israel after 2016.

In my decade working for and with Senator Mathias, I never once heard him suggest that aid to Israel should be tied to Israeli behavior. He was a critic of Israel's invasion of Lebanon in 1982 and of Israel's policy of expanding Jewish settlements in territories occupied in June 1967. These criticisms were grounded in the belief that these actions made peace between Israel and the Palestinians less likely. History has proven him right.

In February 1986, I took my last trip with Senator Mathias—to the Middle East. Some years earlier I had joined the staff of the Senate Committee on Foreign Relations. The senator chaired the Subcommittee on International Economics, which permitted him to focus attention on major economic trends of the period, which he did in a number of oversight hearings. He also was increasingly interested in issues of energy security, which provided one of the reasons to go to the Middle East and specifically to Saudi Arabia. His interest in this particular issue was long standing. He traveled to Mexico in 1977 and 1978 to meet with officials of PEMEX, the Mexican government petroleum agency. As I noted above, he had toured French nuclear facilities. We began our 1986 Middle East trip meeting with Arabian American Oil Company (ARAMCO) officials and flew over oil facilities in the Eastern Province of Saudi Arabia—in the midst of the deadly eight-year war raging between Iraq and Iran just across the Persian Gulf. We also met with the Saudi minister of energy.

Along with Fred Hill, a foreign correspondent for *The Baltimore Sun* before he joined Mathias' personal staff, the three of us traveled for three weeks through Saudi Arabia, Syria, Jordan, Israel and Egypt.

The senator's report on his trip reflected Mathias' view that U.S. "interests are being tested by Soviet probing and, perhaps of greater significance, by anti–Western socio-political forces of considerable weight and vigor." Lebanon remained mired in civil war accompanied by the rise of Hezbollah. Iraq and Iran were still at war, with thousands dying daily a short distance from Saudi Arabia. Mathias had every reason to be disturbed by the direction of events. He emphasized the need for continuing U.S. engagement in the region. Throughout the report and in a subsequent article in *Foreign Policy* magazine, Mathias stressed the need to move forward on the Arab-Israel peace process.[7]

The trip was also a testimony to the high regard that the senator was held in throughout the region despite his being in the final year of his Senate career. The president of Egypt, the prime minister of Israel, the king of Jordan, the energy and defense ministers of Saudi Arabia, the foreign minister of Syria and many, many other senior officials all met with us, as did a cross section of the elite leadership in all these countries.

They all respected the senator's balanced and informed views and his statements and votes on the complex issues at stake. They shared sensitive information and sought his advice. Prime Minister Yitzhak Rabin of Israel even disclosed early warnings of the Iran-Contra scandal, a secret arms-buying scheme in which Israel played a role and which was to roil the Reagan administration. One of the few leaders who decided not to see us was President Hafez al–Assad of Syria—perhaps because he had learned that the senator was carrying a letter from President Reagan concerning American hostages in Lebanon, a country heavily influenced then by Syria.

I was privileged to be associated for the better part of a decade with this truly remarkable public servant.

He was, in important respects, prescient about the future. He wrote, in an extended 1980 piece titled "Toward a New Foreign Policy," that "economic, demographic, political and other forces at work in the world today are reshaping the very environment in which we will have to operate in the 1980s." He also argued that "a successful foreign policy is dependent on successful domestic policies."[8]

But in some respects he was a loner. While he appreciated the benefits of congressional delegations to foreign capitals, he also sought opportunities to travel without Senate colleagues, according to his own schedule, and focused on his own priorities.

I am often asked what distinguished the Senate I worked in from the contemporary Senate and my ready answer is "We had the greatest generation on the floor of the U.S. Senate." These senators (think of Robert Dole, Republican of Kansas, and Daniel Inouye, Democrat of Hawaii, both grievously wounded in combat) had a long view of the national interest and could rise above petty politics when duty to country called. I think too that members got to know each other because they spent more time in Washington and socialized and traveled with each other. Moreover, campaigns were cheaper, so members were not constantly focused on raising money for their next campaign.

Mathias used to say that a Senate term is divided into three parts—the first two years he (she) could be a statesman, the second two he was a senator and the last two he was running for reelection. By the time Mathias left office each of the six years was indistinguishable from the other.

Senate delegation at the Brandenberg Gate, Berlin. Mathias is fifth from right (photograph by Hans Tuch, U.S. Embassy).

Raising massive amounts of money and demonizing opponents became well-trodden paths to electoral victories. The Foreign Relations Committee went from a single, unified, non-partisan staff to separate majority/minority staffs, and increasingly Senate leaderships of both parties were initiating legislation in their offices rather than letting legislation begin in committees and be carefully vetted before proceeding to the floor. Mathias warned that the Senate was becoming dangerously fractured.

Mathias was also disturbed by the constant turnover in executive branch personnel and the appointment of political supporters of the president—Republican and Democrat—to middle level foreign policy positions for which they were not well qualified. He was a strong supporter of the U.S. Foreign Service not just because so many Foreign Service officers resided in his state but because he believed fundamentally in the value of expertise. He frequently grilled ambassadorial appointees who came before the Foreign Relations Committee about their knowledge and expertise and also about to whom they owed their loyalty. Woe to the nominee who suggested it was to the president of the United States and not to the Constitution, the American people and their elected representatives—as their oath dictated.

Perhaps, therefore, it was time for Senator Mathias to leave office. The Reagan administration did not much like him, and the Republican Party was in the process of divesting itself of its moderate members. But what a privilege it was for me to be part of this great man's final decade in office.

NOTES

1. "Senator Mathias Reflects on His Quarter-Century in Congress—Seven Presidential Close-Ups," *The Baltimore Sun*, January 16, 1987.

2. "Observations on the Strategic Arms Limitation Talks," Congressional Record, Tuesday, September 20, 1977.

3. "Official Trip to the Soviet Union by Senator Mathias," Congressional Record, May 10, 1979.

4. "Official Trip to the Soviet Union by Senator Mathias," Congressional Record, May 10, 1979.

5. Gary Rosenblatt, "Mathias and Israel: Where Does He Stand?" *Baltimore Jewish Times*, July 3, 1981.

6. Charles McC. Mathias, Jr., "Ethnic Groups and Foreign Policy," *Foreign Affairs*, Summer 1981.

7. Senator Charles Mathias, "Middle East Trip Report February 5–26–1986: A Report Prepared for the Committee on Foreign Relations of the United States Senate," U.S. Government Printing Office.

8. Senator Charles Mathias, "Toward a New American Foreign Policy," Congressional Record, September 30, 1980.

II. The Rule of Law

Mathias on Grim Outlook for Nixon

FREDERIC B. HILL

Senator Charles McC. Mathias, Jr. (R–MD), one of the first and most outspoken Republican critics of Richard Nixon's behavior and actions as the Watergate scandal unfolded in 1973 and 1974, gave a wide-ranging and clear-eyed assessment of Nixon's crisis to *The Baltimore Sun* in late 1973. Here are excerpts from that interview, November 22, 1973.

* * *

Senator Charles McC. Mathias Jr. (R–MD), believes President Nixon's positive response from Republican congressmen last week will "boomerang" if he does not follow through soon with full disclosure of all Watergate-related information.

Senator Mathias also views the administration's wiretapping, burglary and other illegal acts in the name of national security as "the most troubling of all the Watergate matters."

Question: Is there sufficient evidence to bring impeachment charges against the President?

Answer: As a member of the Senate who would be a constitutional member of the court trying the impeachment charge, I think it would be extremely improper to comment on whether there is evidence to sustain a charge.

I think this, however. That impeachment, unlike a criminal case, is composed of several elements, evidence and legal culpability, but also political elements, questions of policy, and the ultimate question of the welfare of the country which are all not present in criminal cases.[1]

Q: What bothers you most about everything that's happened in the Watergate spectrum of events?

(From left) Senator Mathias, Senator J. Glenn Beall (R–MD), President Nixon, and Representative Goodloe Byron (D–MD) on the campaign trail, 1972 (Mathias Family).

A: I think the [White House] plan for extra-legal surveillance in many ways is the most troubling of all the individual actions that have taken place. One, because the President felt obliged for five days to sanction a plan that was a thrust at the very vitals of the Constitution and the Bill of Rights.

And I think it's necessary before this is all over that we understand what his perception of the threats to national security were that demanded this drastic step, and equally important, what were the weaknesses in the statutory law enforcement agencies that required the recruitment of the "plumbers" to carry out the plan.

Q: *Did you ask the President Wednesday for an explanation?*

A: I did, and he promised he would give me a written statement of his position.

Q: *On the Today show [Wednesday], you said there was "an air of fantasy" about the meetings with the President this week. Would you elaborate?*

A: Yes, it is an extraordinary experience in which you sit in a room with the President of the United States and hear the range of criticism and comment and counsel which were directed to him—in which his best friends in the room were urging him to act with humility and drop his aggressive stance.

These are not the kinds of conversations that usually take place between presidents and senators. These are not discussions about legislation and national policy. This was a very fundamental discussion that must be very rare in all history.

Q: You also compared the meeting with events that led up to the signing of the Magna Carta. Did you mean to compare the President and King John, or were you referring to the overall context of the situation?

A: I was only talking about the atmosphere, the setting, in which a chief of state is surrounded by those who advise and consent and who are telling him, really, what has to be done in the reform of his government if it is to survive.

Q: Do you feel if the President had not been elected by such a margin and there was a vice president in office, with all the charges, the involvement of so many of his top aides in wrongdoing, that he would still be in office?

A: It's very useful to him and his staff to be able to point to the landslide proportions of the '72 victory. I don't think it's critical though. I think the events that have taken place in the year since the '72 victory are so catastrophic that there isn't any credit left in the bank.

Q: Do you think this golden opportunity for election reform is going to go by the boards because of entrenched opposition in Congress?

A: Let me say I don't think Congress should adjourn until it has actually sent to the President a major election reform bill. If you're ever going to need a graphic illustration of why we have to change, this is the time: High officials, either fired or resigned or under indictment or sometimes all three, largely traced to electoral difficulties. It would be a serious indictment of the Congress if we let the technical difficulties of legislating in controversial areas prevent us from getting this job done.

Q: Some congressmen said they felt the President still views criticism of his Watergate handling as largely partisan. Do you feel that is true or do you think he is now interested in getting the whole truth out?

A: [The meeting] included some Republicans who [are] his closest and most firm supporters. I don't believe there was a single person who didn't have some criticism and some advice, so if he had any concept that this was all generated by Democrats, that idea would have been disabused.

People have been pretty frank, [and] if this appears to be only a one-shot effort that is not followed up, that it will in fact turn out to be a boomerang.

"YOU'RE BARKING UP THE WRONG TREE."

"You're Barking up the Wrong Tree" (Neil Grauer, *Baltimore News-American*, 1974; Johns Hopkins University Special Collections).

Q: Do you think the President will escape impeachment if the question is not resolved fairly soon?

A: Events will govern that. If we've heard the last bombshells, no more bad news, that's one thing. If there are more disclosures, more bombshells, that's another. That's why I feel it's absolutely necessary to have full disclosure and find out what we're dealing with.

Q: What do you think the President needs to do?

A: The first step he needs to take is to make available all the physical evidence that's pertinent, and I don't think he can make the threshold decision as to what's pertinent. I think that all the tapes, the documents, other physical evidence need to be turned over.

Then you can look at what it is, and make some judgment as to whether questions and answers, or some public forum would be appropriate to get his personal knowledge.

Q: Do you think the administration's Watergate problems have contributed to other foreign and domestic troubles?

A: I really feel that through the summer and fall the government has run with a remarkable degree of stability. I would have to say, however, that with the "Saturday Night Massacre" [the firing of Archibald Cox, the special Watergate prosecutor, and the resignation of Elliot L. Richardson, the attorney general, etc.], that something changed, and that we are entering a period when Watergate is creating such a major concentration of interest that it is threatening other things.

Responsible public servants look over their shoulders three times before they say anything; public service is being affected ... and the only way to resolve this is the kind of disclosure I told White House aides we ought to have had back in the summer.

Postscript: Dozens of more damning disclosures continued; Mathias gave a long floor speech and subsequent interview in December 1973 charging that the Nixon administration was leading the nation down the road to dictatorship. The Supreme Court ruled that Nixon must turn over tape recordings which confirmed his deep participation in Watergate and its cover-up and the House of Representatives began impeachment proceedings. Facing certain impeachment, told by Republican senators Barry Goldwater of Arizona and Hugh Scott of Pennsylvania to go, Richard M. Nixon, the 37th president of the United States, resigned on August 8, 1974.

Note

1. https://www.proquest.com/historical-newspapers/mathias-predicts-gop-shift-if-nixon-withholds/docview/536138940/se-2.

Standing Alone Against Fear

Steven J. Metalitz

In recent years, the problem of mass incarceration has emerged as a critical issue in criminal justice reform. Criminologists, legal experts and a growing number of political figures in both parties have decried the social and economic costs of a system that locks up too many people for too long, especially for nonviolent offenses such as drug possession, and that disproportionately burdens communities of color.

Although the historical roots of over-incarceration are complex, one key inflection point occurred in 1984, when Congress stripped federal judges of nearly all their discretion to craft sentences for convicted federal offenders that reflected the specific crimes committed by the specific individuals before them. Instead, judges were required to impose sentences within a range of "guidelines" which, despite their label, were intended to be mandatory in nearly all cases. The same legislation abolished parole for federal prisoners.

Many independent analysts warned at the time that these reforms were likely to result in longer sentences in federal criminal cases and a burgeoning federal prison population. Congress turned a deaf ear to these warnings. Indeed, only one U.S. senator was sufficiently concerned about the unintended impacts of federal sentencing reforms to oppose them publicly: Senator Charles McC. Mathias, Jr.

As one of Mathias' counsels on the Senate Judiciary Committee staff, I had a front row seat for some of this drama. Today, when the damage inflicted on our society by policies of mass incarceration is more clearly understood, it's worth a look back at Mathias' lonely—and unsuccessful— quest to divert the legislative juggernaut from its path.

* * *

The genesis of the 1984 federal sentencing law can be found in the proposed omnibus federal criminal code—the infamous S. 1—first proposed in the 1970s. But the drive toward tougher federal sentencing picked up momentum after the 1980 landslide election that not only brought Ronald Reagan into the White House but also handed Republicans control of the U.S. Senate for the first time in decades. The seismic tremors of this legislative earthquake transformed the landscape of federal policy, notably on the range of social issues falling within the jurisdiction of the Senate Judiciary Committee.

The committee's ranking Republican before the 1980 election, Strom Thurmond of South Carolina, was expected to exercise his seniority to chair the Armed Services Committee, to help enact the accelerated military spending on which Reagan had campaigned. Mathias, who was easily re-elected to his third term in 1980, was the next most senior Republican member of Judiciary and was poised to take that gavel. But Thurmond chose to assume the Judiciary chairmanship, and the new committee majority was packed with arch-conservative freshmen to help Thurmond advance Reagan's conservative social agenda. Mathias, then seen as a liberal maverick by the GOP establishment, was relegated to the chairmanship of the Criminal Law Subcommittee.

Tough-on-crime measures were an important feature of Reagan's law-and-order agenda. Some of the proposals, which implicated fundamental constitutional issues, attracted sufficient opposition among Democrats and moderate Republicans that they did not advance. However, on a broad swath of anti-crime measures, the Reagan Republicans garnered enthusiastic support from many Democrats, including the new ranking member of the Criminal Law subcommittee, young Joseph Biden of Delaware, then in his second Senate term. During the 2020 presidential campaign, Biden was confronted with his leading role in enacting the draconian sentencing provisions of the 1994 crime bill, but in fact his support for tough sentencing measures was evident much earlier.

Wary of Mathias' skepticism about many elements of the crime package, chairman Thurmond kept some of them away from the Criminal Law subcommittee, often holding hearings in other subcommittees and sometimes relying on the legislative record compiled in previous Congresses. Thus, when the Violent Crime and Drug Enforcement Improvements Act came to the Senate floor on September 30, 1982, the bill had never formally been considered in the Judiciary Committee at all. Nonetheless, with 64 senators listed as co-sponsors, including 25 Democrats, its ultimate passage was virtually assured. Mathias was well aware of this when he came to the floor that day, but he was determined to make the case against what he considered the most problematic aspect of the bill—its sentencing reform provisions.[1]

Mathias' basic concern was that a move toward determinate sentencing under inflexible guidelines, accompanied by the abolition of parole, would inevitably lead to longer federal criminal sentences and thus to overcrowding in the federal prison system. On the Senate floor, he called the bill a "budget buster" that would "probably double the population of the federal prisons." He noted that 80 percent of state prison systems were then under court orders to deal with overcrowding. "Here we are doing something which we know is going to make things worse in Federal prisons," he concluded.

Since this was an era in which, unlike today, substantive issues were sometimes actually debated and voted on in the Senate, Mathias' arguments were parried at some length by Biden, the Democratic floor manager for the legislation, who concluded, "I do not think it can be presumed … that there will be longer sentences." Mathias extracted from Biden a statement that the bill was not intended to lengthen average sentences. Then Mathias' amendment to strike all the sentencing reform proposals from the bill was put to a voice vote. As expected, it failed.

Mathias felt strongly enough that the federal sentencing reform was fundamentally flawed that when the bill came to a vote on final passage later that day, he stood alone to vote no. The final tally: 95 to 1. The bill was sent to the House, which stripped out the sentencing reforms and, as adjournment loomed, sent the bill back to the Senate as a take it or leave it proposition. The Senate acquiesced in the slimmed-down bill, but in the end, Reagan vetoed it.[2] Thus, Mathias' solitary opposition prevailed in this first round of the fight over federal sentencing policy, but, of course, the vastly stronger forces pushing for determinate sentencing lived to fight another day.

That day arrived soon. On July 21, 1983, the Senate Judiciary Committee took up the Comprehensive Crime Control Act of 1983. Its sentencing reform provisions were essentially identical to those the

A characteristic gesture, standing alone against a comprehensive crime bill (Mathias Family).

Senate had passed the previous year, so Mathias was clear-eyed about the fate of the amendments he offered at the Judiciary Committee mark-up and later on the Senate floor. But the arguments he made in his minority report on the legislation in the committee, and in the floor debates a few months later, were remarkably prescient about the problematic consequences of the legislation.[3]

Mathias took a more targeted approach than he had the previous year. One of his amendments accepted the general idea of sentencing guidelines but gave the job of drawing them up to the federal judges themselves or, more precisely, to a commission (to include some non-judges) to be formed within the judicial branch. Mathias felt strongly that the federal judges who presided over trials or pleas at which defendants were convicted of federal crimes were best positioned to tailor sentences to the particular defendant and to his or her crimes. If, as Mathias conceded, the results sometimes lacked consistency or appeared arbitrary, the judges themselves should be the ones to develop guidelines aimed at achieving greater coherence.

Mathias' views were strongly influenced by conversations with Judge Frank Kaufman, chief judge of the U.S. District Court for Maryland. Kaufman, like many other federal judges, strongly objected to the idea of legislation that would, as Mathias put it in his minority report, "consign [judges] to the task of operating a sentencing decision machine designed and built by somebody else."

When the bill came to the Senate floor on January 30, 1984, Mathias urged senators to "listen very carefully to the judges, to the people who have a daily experience in this most difficult of human activities, the sentencing of other humans." And in offering this amendment on the Senate floor the next day, he asked, "Does it make any sense to present the bench with a fait accompli and tell the judges, 'go on and administer the guidelines that have been drawn up for you'? Would it not be more sensible to enlist the skill, experience, knowledge and cooperation of the judges in the first place?"

Mathias also reprised the theme that had been a focus of his opposition in 1982: the likelihood that the legislation would lead to further overcrowding of the federal prisons—or, in modern terms, to over-incarceration. One amendment he proposed in committee directly confronted this risk by directing the Sentencing Commission to "insure that its sentencing guidelines would not be likely to result in an increase in aggregate or overall average term of imprisonment, or in the federal prison population." After this amendment failed by a 15–1 vote, Mathias' minority statement lamented that the bill "would do absolutely nothing to reverse the alarming trend toward more and more indiscriminate use of incarceration in the federal prisons, which are already bulging with their highest populations in history." Before the full Senate, Mathias sought to "protect against overreliance on incarceration" by calling for courts to "impose the least severe appropriate sanction" warranted by the facts of the case and to "order imprisonment only if no other sanction is adequate to achieve the purpose of sentencing."

Biden, who again in 1984 led the debate for the Democrats, conceded that the adoption of sentencing guidelines "could under certain circumstances increase the prison population" but went on to "argue that the opposite is just as likely to occur." Mathias agreed that "it was impossible to predict what will happen" but noted as a "straw in the wind" the fact that "private corporations, organized for profit, organized to make money, see an opportunity here. They are so sure that the prison population is going to increase that they have blueprints drawn and are ready to put up prisons for rent, cells for hire." Biden, at first apparently not taking the issue seriously, inquired whether these businesses were building the cells "for their employees." Later in the debate, though, Biden responded that the entry of private businesses into prison construction and operation "does not necessarily mean that we shall need additional space" but could simply represent an opportunity to achieve greater efficiency through privatization. Nevertheless, Mathias presciently brought to the fore the rise of private prisons, which many experts now see as a key enabler of policies of over-incarceration.

On the Senate floor, Mathias also focused on two other fundamental flaws with rigid sentencing guidelines. One he had flagged in his minority report at the Judiciary Committee: that "by drastically reducing judicial discretion in sentencing, Title II in no way eliminates discretion from the system. It merely displaces it from the courtroom, where it is exercised under the scrutiny of the public, to other venues."

Here, Mathias accurately predicted precisely what happened in the federal system: The decisions by prosecutors, made behind closed doors, of what crimes to charge, and what plea bargains to accept, had a far greater impact on the sentences defendants ultimately received than the decisions announced by judges, highly constrained by the guidelines, in open court.

Mathias also warned that any progress toward less disparate sentencing decisions that guidelines could provide could easily be undermined, or eliminated altogether, by subsequent legislative decisions to impose mandatory minimum sentences for certain offenses. He asked his colleagues, "Are we ready to take a pledge to refrain from legislation that would unbalance the very delicate calculations that the U.S. Sentencing Commission would make? … I think the answer is clearly that we will not take that pledge." Events in the very next Congress showed that Mathias' prediction was correct.

Finally, Mathias appealed to conservative principles that his colleagues on both sides of the aisle appeared eager to jettison in the rush to position themselves as "tough on crime." He again denounced the bill as a "budget buster" that would create "another federal bureaucracy with a sweeping charter to impose solutions for problems which may not really exist." His closing peroration on the floor on January 31 noted that "the violent street crime which haunts the inhabitants of our inner cities … must be combated primarily at the local level," not through sweeping federal legislation. In effect, Mathias cast himself as a true conservative in William F. Buckley's famous description, "standing athwart history, yelling, 'Stop!'"[4]

Of course, history did not stop. Mathias demanded a roll call vote on only one of his amendments; it was defeated 76–1. The others were rejected by voice vote. On February 2, 1984, the Senate adopted the federal sentencing reform measure by a vote of 91–1, and it was ultimately signed into law by President Reagan.[5] Mathias' closing statement in the debate struck themes that ring true in today's debates over criminal justice reform:

> Mr. President, it may be that on my dissenting vote … I will stand alone in the U.S. Senate. I have stood alone in this Chamber before on this issue; perhaps I will again. But I am heartened by the fact that the consensus in the Senate in support of this unwise legislation is not reflected in the country as a whole. In many circles—among criminal justice experts, among the judiciary, among civil libertarians, among religious and social action organizations, among concerned citizens of all kinds—the voices of dissent are growing stronger.....
>
> I believe we must acknowledge that this bill owes much of its support to fear. Violent crime plagues America; but the fear of crime tortures our people. Wherever the cold fingers of fear have insinuated themselves, we feel that we cannot rest until we have done something—anything—to strike back at what frightens us. Sometimes it seems as though the bigger and more dramatic the action that we take, the more we can reassure ourselves that we are doing something useful.
>
> This syndrome is at work here in the U.S. Senate. We act as though the bigger the crime bill we pass, the more we are doing to fight crime. We are now about to add another 400 pages of legislation to the United States Code. The proponents consider this only a modest step, since this bill's predecessors were twice as long. Our fears tell us that any response this massive must be a good one.
>
> Mr. President, if we would stop to think about it, we all know better than that. The dramatic gesture, the mammoth bill, will not win the fight against crime. Only the patient honest efforts of our law-abiding citizens, who do not like what violent crime is doing to their communities, are likely to have a major impact. The war against crime must be fought—and won—gradually and incrementally. Success depends on steady progress more than on dramatic breakthroughs. The help which the American people need from the Congress

may include some incremental changes in the federal criminal laws. But most of all the American people need a realistic, effective justice assistance program to aid their efforts at the local level. What the American people do not need is blockbuster legislation like S. 1762.[6]

* * *

The postscript to this story was not long in coming. In September of 1986, with mid-term elections looming, Congress once again found itself caught up in a legislative frenzy over crime—specifically, over drug crime. The immediate precipitating event was the shocking drug overdose death of University of Maryland basketball phenom Len Bias. Coming the day after Bias had been drafted by the Boston Celtics of the NBA, his death made national headlines and impelled the Democratic-controlled House to speedily adopt another "mammoth bill" to assuage the nation's fears. The Anti-Drug Abuse Act of 1986 was then sent to the Senate, which held no committee hearings or mark-up on it. After three weeks of intense informal negotiations between the House and Senate, the bill was enacted on October 17, 1986.[7]

The 1986 bill fulfilled Mathias' 1984 prediction that Congress, in its eagerness to position itself as tough on crime, would not "stay its hand" on sentencing policy to give the recently enacted guidelines system a chance to achieve their goal of reducing sentencing disparities. Instead, the 1986 legislation included a smorgasbord of mandatory minimum sentences for various federal drug crimes. Most infamously, it imposed the same penalties for possession of crack cocaine (believed to be used disproportionately by Black people) as applied to possession of one hundred times that amount of powdered cocaine (believed to be consumed by more White people). This crack-powder sentencing disparity soon became the poster child for the charge of systemic racism in the criminal justice system.

Ultimately, the 1986 legislation, along with subsequent legislative enactments of tougher sentencing, doomed the stated intentions of the proponents of sentencing reform that it would not lead to a massive increase in the federal prison population. In 1984, there were fewer than 36,000 federal prisoners; that tally doubled in seven years. It peaked two decades later at more than 219,000. Mathias, as it turned out, foresaw the future far better than Biden did.[8]

The debate over the 1986 drug bill unfolded over Mathias' final weeks in office. When the House bill came over to the Senate, Mathias was among the leading voices urging caution. On September 26, 1986, he came to the floor to reprise some of the same concerns that animated his 1984 speech. Acknowledging that drug abuse was a "very serious problem," he warned that "in our haste to do something about drugs before the end of this session of Congress … we are in danger of doing what Alexis de Toc-queville warned us against 150 years ago: 'flattering the passions.' Because when we flatter the passions, we are in danger of forgetting fundamental principles." But ultimately, Mathias supported the final legislative prod-uct. When the Senate finally passed the bill 97–2, Mathias voted yes.

What happened? Several factors were in play. As adjournment neared, the drug bill became a proverbial "Christmas tree" from which many other legislative ornaments dangled. One of these was a landmark Mathias bill in the field of privacy and information policy: the Electronic Commu-nications Privacy Act. The opportunity to enact this first legislative pro-tection for the privacy of e-mail communications, which Mathias crafted along with Vermont Democrat Patrick Leahy, provided a fitting capstone to Mathias' long-standing commitment to updating federal law to meet the challenges of new technology. With Mathias on the verge of retirement from the Senate, the drug bill was the only vehicle available to leave his mark on electronic information policy.[9]

The main reason, though, was that Mathias' attention was focused on what he viewed as an even greater danger than the continued slide toward over-incarceration. The 1982 and 1984 crime bills passed easily in the Sen-ate because they had been stripped of some of the most radical elements of the Reagan-era criminal justice agenda. In the legislative cauldron of 1986, heated to the boiling point by Bias' death and the perceived popu-lar demand to crack down on illegal drugs, these more drastic propos-als received broader support. The bill the Senate received from the House would have allowed some illegally seized evidence to be used in federal court; required that U.S. military forces be conscripted into the war on drugs; and brought back the federal death penalty (which the Supreme Court had struck down in 1972). Mathias and his allies, notably Michigan Democrat Carl Levin, made it clear to the Senate leaders that they were prepared to filibuster the entire bill if these provisions remained in it.

Negotiations off the Senate floor resulted in a face-saving deal. The three most controversial provisions were excised from the bill. Their pro-ponents were given the opportunity to offer amendments reinstating them. The next day, Senator Mack Mattingly (R–GA) offered the death penalty amendment. In a test vote, 25 senators—including Mathias and nine other Republicans—opposed it. Mattingly, stating his "understand-ing that the opposition would filibuster and kill this vital bill," withdrew his amendment. The maneuver allowed Mattingly and other senators up for re-election to tell the voters they had stood up and called for drug deal-ers to be executed for their crimes, but the bill as sent back to the House contained no death penalty provisions.

That was not the end of the story, however. In the heat of the moment, the House, normally the less draconian of the two houses on criminal justice policy, insisted on re-inserting federal capital punishment into the bill and deposited its revised bill on the Senate's doorstep just weeks before Election Day. Faced with a filibuster threat, the Senate leadership called for a vote to cut off further debate. On October 15, the cloture motion garnered 58 votes, two short of the 60 required to prevent a filibuster. Majority Leader Bob Dole immediately called a meeting of the chief protagonists in his office to work out a way forward.

A *Washington Post* article a few days later describes what happened next:

> Closeted in [Dole's] ornate office, the death penalty opponents and backers fought for ground as Mathias straddled a chair and quietly hung on the edges of debate. Finally, sliding forward on the chair as if he were riding a horse, Mathias moved in and made his point.
>
> "If you're asking whether or not I will filibuster, if the death penalty stays in that bill," Mathias warned, "I say to you, I am prepared to spend Christmas here."
>
> Everyone knew he meant it, said Biden, and within minutes the death penalty provision was buried. "It would be the way Mac would love to go out."[10]

On the eve of adjournment, the 1986 drug bill was sent back to the House and ultimately enacted with no death penalty provisions. In the closing days of his 18-year Senate tenure, Mathias' yelling "Stop!" had succeeded. The next time Congress indulged in its election year ritual of pandering to "tough-on-crime" sentiment, Mathias was gone, and the federal death penalty was reinstated after a 16-year hiatus.[11] But the Maryland Republican's valedictory warning, spoken on the Senate floor on September 26, 1986, rings even truer today:

> We simply must not be slaves to the moment or instruments of our passions. It would be the ultimate folly to sacrifice our liberties and imperil vital health programs, only to discover that the drug crisis has not abated. If we are contemplating changes to important individual freedoms, if we are about to alter major social commitments, then those modifications simply must be discussed fully. They must be understood totally. The consequences must be anticipated.

NOTES

1. Mathias' participation in the Senate floor debate on the bill S. 2572 can be found in the Congressional Record for September 30, 1982, at pp. 26535–26541. The vote on final passage can be found at p. 26581.

2. In part, Reagan justified the veto because the bill presented to him failed to "address sentencing reform." The veto message included a statement of the president's "strong support" for the bill passed by the Senate, over Mathias' objection. "Memorandum Returning Without Approval a Bill Concerning Contract Services for Drug Dependent Federal

Offenders," January 14, 1983, viewed at https://www.presidency.ucsb.edu/documents/memorandum-returning-without-approval-bill-concerning-contract-services-for-drug-dependent.

3. S. 1762, 98th Congress. For the Judiciary Committee proceedings on the bill, see the Senate Judiciary Committee report, S. Rpt. 98–225 (September 14, 1983). Mathias' minority views are on p. 782, and the votes on amendments he offered in committee are on pp. 423–24. For Mathias' participation in the Senate floor debate, see the Congressional Record for January 30, 1984, beginning at p. 837, and January 31, 1984, beginning at p. S522.

4. William F. Buckley, Jr., "Our Mission Statement," November 19, 1955, https://www.nationalreview.com/1955/11/our-mission-statement-william-f-buckley-jr/.

5. Public Law 98–473 (October 12, 1984). More than 20 years later, the U.S. Supreme Court struck down, as violative of the Sixth Amendment right to jury trial, the provision of the 1984 law that made the guidelines mandatory. By declaring that this provision must be "severed and excised" from the statute, the Supreme Court rendered the guidelines "effectively advisory." *United States v. Booker*, 543 U.S. 220 (2005). Of course, if the legislation before the Senate in 1984 had proposed advisory rather than mandatory guidelines, Mathias' approach to the bill would have been far different.

6. Congressional Record, January 31, 1984, at p. S570.

7. For a detailed narrative chronology of the Anti-Drug Abuse Act of 1986, see https://www.thecongressproject.com/anti-drug-abuse-act-of-1986 . For Mathias' remarks on the Senate floor, see the Congressional Record for September 26, 1986, at p. 26462, and September 27, 1986, at p. 26752.

8. Federal Bureau of Prisons population statistics, https://www.bop.gov/mobile/about/population_statistics.jsp.

9. The Electronic Communications Privacy Act was ultimately enacted as Public Law 99–508.

10. Saundra Saperstein, "Mathias: Warrior in Minority," *The Washington Post*, OctOBeR 19, 1986, p. A1.

11. Capital punishment was restored for a limited number of federal crimes in the Anti-Drug Abuse Act of 1988, Pub. L. 100–690, and was greatly expanded by the Violent Crime Control and Law Enforcement Act of 1994, Pub. L. 103–322.

His Conscience Was His Guide

Rep. Steny Hoyer

When I first arrived in the House as a freshman representing Maryland's Fifth District in 1981, one of those who welcomed me was our state's senior senator, Mac Mathias. I had first met him years before I took office, when I was interning on Capitol Hill for then–Congressman and later Senator Daniel Brewster. Mathias had been Brewster's law school roommate, longtime friend, and the man who would ultimately unseat him in the 1968 campaign. I found Mathias at that time to be an exceptionally gracious and principled man, an exemplar of what a public official ought to be. In particular, I admired his commitment to civil rights and fair housing, issues that would be the hallmark of my own campaign in 1966 for State Senate.

After he welcomed me to Congress, Mathias continually proved my initial assessments correct. He was a man of grace, of conviction, of high political acumen and one who had genuine respect for the office he held and the institution in which he served. His belief in the importance and power of public service was matched by his love of Maryland and its people.

Mathias had great faith in the Constitution, in the protection of civil rights, in the need to safeguard our environment, and in the necessity of curbing the corrupting influence of money in our politics. He wanted to see the United States enact foreign policies that earned us respect around the world. Mathias wouldn't stray from those principles for anything, even if it meant voting differently than his Republican colleagues. And he frequently did.

It was clear to all of us who served with him—and to the Marylanders who voted for him time and again—that the letter next to Mathias' name was never the primary factor in his decision-making. When it came to legislation, he closely examined the merits and the costs of its implementation. He asked whether it would, on the whole, make our nation stronger

98

and safer, bring opportunity to American businesses and workers, and leave our country and our planet cleaner and healthier for future generations. These questions mattered far more to him than that of which party's legislators had written the bill or which side pushed for its adoption.

For these reasons, he and I often aligned on key pieces of legislation in the five years we overlapped in Congress, despite being on opposite sides of the aisle. On the environment, we shared a commitment to cleaning up the Chesapeake Bay and safeguarding our land, air and water against pollution. On civil rights, we fought for fair housing legislation, saw to it that Martin Luther King, Jr., would be honored with a national holiday, and sanctioned those responsible for apartheid in South Africa. Our work together on these issues was guided by principle, not by party.

Mathias wasn't naïve, though—he understood that there was a political cost to this bipartisanship. In 1981, he was denied the chairmanship of the Judiciary Committee after Senator Strom Thurmond and other conservatives played a malign game of musical chairs to prevent him from bringing his commitment to civil rights to that powerful position. This incident wasn't an anomaly; during his tenure, Mathias frustrated more than a few members of his own party, and he paid a political price for it, which may have included his prospects for running for the presidency in the 1970s. But where many would have backed down, chosen short-term gain and influence over principle, Mathias stuck to his guns. Even while generally going along with President Reagan's economic agenda in the 1980s, Mathias never hesitated to buck his own party on critical social and human rights issues. He always felt that his political sacrifices were worth it. History has shown they were.

To be a legislator of that ilk takes guts. It also requires composure and grace. Even when Mathias and I found ourselves on the opposite side of an issue, I always had tremendous respect for him, a result of his geniality and candor. "Politician" did not adequately describe him; Mathias was truly a *statesman*.

Crucially, however, he wasn't alone in that regard. Mac Mathias was a good man, a good senator, but he was not alone. In those days, Republicans like him, like Jacob Javits of New York and Clifford Case of New Jersey, voted their conscience and regularly crossed the aisle to legislate effectively with their Democratic colleagues while Republicans were in the minority.

That's because Mathias and his colleagues understood that crucial to the survival and success of our democracy is a loyal opposition. When I speculate about how he and those like him would characterize the Senate today, I suspect they would be aghast at how much Republican senators' individual judgment has yielded to unquestioning fealty to their party and the individual who has taken it in his thrall. When we look at moments of defiance and bipartisanship among Republican senators now, such acts of exception shine powerfully through the darkness.

How sad it is that Mathias' party now follows a man who is the very antithesis of everything he represented. Surely, our nation's divisions and how they have been manifested in the halls of the Capitol, most nightmarishly on January 6, would horrify him. Mathias would be the first to say that the Senate needs a responsible minority, loyal to America and its people, in order to hold the majority accountable, working with Democrats when they can and opposing them when they must.

At a time when politicians too often legislate to the worst instincts of the electorate, seeking short-term political gains at the expense of the long-term well-being of our constituents and our country, we would do well to reflect on the legacies of lawmakers like Mathias. He was a man who wanted to represent the best of Maryland, the best of America, to legislate to their highest principles and most noble aspirations.

All hope, however, is not lost. Though it may be difficult at first glance to pick them out of the crowd, there remain people of goodwill and decency and comity in the Republican Party in both the House and Senate who are still hoping to work across the aisle and looking for opportunities to put their country first. I pray that they succeed, that they can draw on the strength and wisdom of forebears like Mac Mathias to take a stand for fundamental American principles around which we can and must unite: civil rights, rule of law, democracy, patriotism and mutual respect. I hope that these Republicans will embrace the ways of Mac Mathias publicly, not only in their hearts and within the confines of their private offices. Our democracy will be at risk if Republicans of good will and good sense remain silent.

Particularly in times of great division, all of us—Democrats and Republicans alike—could do with a reminder that our responsibility to those we represent must always serve as our guiding light. Mathias believed strongly that it was his duty to Marylanders to work across the aisle whenever doing so served their interests. Governing responsibly for the people, regardless of the politics of the day and electoral machinations—that was what he always did and would exhort us all to do now. In the minority for most of his time in the Senate, he knew that his party's role wasn't to gin up gridlock in order to foment dissatisfaction with the majority party. That wouldn't do anything to help Marylanders see justice done or their lives improved.

Every two years, I welcome a new class of freshmen to Congress with a dinner and a candlelit tour of the Capitol. At the end of the evening, I tell them that, as they endeavor to serve with conviction, they will be constantly tested, confronted with differing opinions and conflicting priorities. When this inevitably happens, their conscience must be their guide. I leave them with my favorite lines of wisdom from Edmund Burke, the 18th-century parliamentarian who expressed so eloquently the responsibilities of a legislator:

> It ought to be the happiness and glory of a representative to live in the strictest union, the closest correspondence, and most unreserved communication with his constituents.... It is his duty to sacrifice his repose, his pleasures, his satisfactions, to theirs; and above all, ever, and in all cases, to prefer their interest to his own.
>
> But his unbiased opinion, his mature judgment, his enlightened sense of conscience, he ought not to sacrifice you, to any man, or to any set of men living.... Your representative owes you, not his industry only, but his judgment; and he betrays, instead of serving you, if he sacrifices it to your opinion.

Mac Mathias, who often cited Burke's wise words as well, never sacrificed his judgment to opinion—and surely would not counsel others to do so. He neither failed to rely on his conscience nor draw on his wisdom and experience in staking out his positions. Yet he remained always in the closest bonds of trust with the people of our state and worked his hardest to ensure that they always came along with him after he made the strongest possible case for his view. As so many of us who worked alongside him recognized, Mac Mathias was a legislator, a politician, and a leader *par excellence*.

His legacy surrounds us still. In our home state of Maryland, which he so loved, he is remembered for his efforts to clean up the Chesapeake Bay and its watershed. Communities across our country may not have streets named after him, but they are paved with opportunities more equally accessible because of the civil rights policies he championed. Children born today in South Africa enjoy freedom and human rights because he stood against his own party leadership to demand a tough stance against apartheid.

I sometimes wonder what Congress would look like today if Mac Mathias were still walking these halls in his signature crumpled suit. Even though he is no longer with us, we can still maintain his presence by following in his example. I hope that he will serve as a model to American legislators for many decades to come, inspiring us all to continue striving toward greater consensus, civility, and mutual respect even as we advocate opposing views on the issues. If we can each find a measure of Mathias's courage to stand up for what is right and of his loyalty to country over party, we may, by the light of his example, chart a path out of the present darkness and into a brighter tomorrow.

Ordered Liberty

Senator Mathias' View of the Constitution

RANDOLPH MARSHALL COLLINS

On a fall day in 1986, Senator Mathias summoned me to the U.S. Senate floor. The senator had announced about a year before that he would not seek reelection, a disappointing decision for me. Like all those who worked for him, I admired his public service and wanted to see him continue. When I got to the Senate chamber, the senator was standing on the floor just in front of the marble dais where the presiding officer sits. He turned and greeted me with a smile, exclaiming, "Philosopher," a nickname he sometimes used for me. He explained that he'd asked me there because an important anniversary was fast approaching: the 200th anniversary of the drafting of the U.S. Constitution on September 17, 1787.

The senator was a serious history buff, so it wasn't surprising that the birthday of the U.S. Constitution would be on his mind. In this case he wanted me to draft an article for the *University of Maryland Law Review* for the Constitution's commemoration.[1] I asked him what sort of approach he wanted to take to commemorate our founding document. At this point, he stopped and stared at me with the silent, unreadable expression he often displayed when he was in thought. To me and others who worked for him, this stone-silent stare was always a bit disconcerting. It was if the sound of my question had failed to reach him, or perhaps just the speed of sound was slower than usual.

After a few quiet moments, Senator Mathias told me that Attorney General Ed Meese had expounded a theory of constitutional interpretation called "original intent" or "originalism," which he wanted to discuss in upcoming speeches and the law review article. Originalism is the theory that the meaning of the Constitution is the meaning that existed at the time of its drafting or ratification—which meant that any growth or evolution in the law since then was simply not applicable. At the time Mathias

102

and I met on the Senate floor, originalism was in its infancy.[2] But its influence would grow steadily until today, when a third of the justices on the U.S. Supreme Court explicitly endorse its use and numerous lower courts use it for divining the meaning of the Constitution. Indeed, Justices Clarence Thomas, Neil Gorsuch and Amy Coney Barrett all say they use this method to decide what the Constitution means.[3]

Former Justice Antonin Scalia did, too. So Mathias' focus on this way of interpreting the Constitution is even more relevant now than when he began addressing it more than 38 years ago.

Constitutional interpretation is crucial for applying the document's intentionally broad phrases. The document's nearly 8,000 words are rife with ambiguities. What do "due process," "equal protection," "cruel and unusual punishment" or even "freedom of speech" actually mean? Over the centuries, these provisions have been interpreted in numerous, often contradictory ways. As Senator Mathias would write, the Constitution in some cases was a "map without a legend," failing to tell us how it should be decoded. Does money equate with speech, so that restrictions on corporate campaign contributions violate the First Amendment? Is it a "reasonable search" for police to obtain a blood sample for a DNA test from a criminal defendant without first getting a warrant? And when the First Amendment states "Congress shall make no law … prohibiting … the freedom of speech," does this phrase also forbid any federal official such as the president from restricting free speech rights? Or is its application only—as the First Amendment literally states—just to Congress? All these inquiries and many more entail deciding what the Constitution actually means.

Advocates of originalism such as former attorney general Meese argued that to deal with the Constitution's ambiguity, its meaning must be fixed by the original intent of those who wrote or ratified the Constitution and its 27 subsequent amendments. Adherents of this view take comfort in the certainty that the static meaning originalism provides in the face of historical changes or evolutions in legal precedent. Originalism claims to provide a neutral interpretive method that constrains judges and others from attempting to insert their own personal biases.[4]

Moreover, supporters of originalism argue that it derives its legal authority from the principles in contract law. When parties enter a contract, a "meeting of the minds" must occur when a legal agreement is reached. If there is a contract dispute, the parties must abide by agreement's intent. Similarly, our Constitution is said to be like a contract. To use the British philosopher John Locke's term, it is a "social contract." Therefore, disagreements over its meaning should be resolved by reference only to the intent of the founders and/or drafters as well as those who ratified it or any of its amendments.

Senator Mathias pointed out significant problems with originalism, starting with whose original intent should be used for guidance. Should we look to the 55 delegates who had a hand in drafting the Constitution and, if so, which of the delegates—Madison, Adams, Franklin, Hamilton, etc.? Madison and Hamilton, for example, disagreed over whether the Constitution empowered Congress to establish the first national bank. Madison relied upon the absence of any explicit Constitutional reference to a bank in Congress' enumerated powers. Hamilton, on the other hand, looked to the implied powers Congress possessed, including the "necessary and proper" clause.

Senator Mathias pointed out he was himself a ratifier for Maryland of the 14th Amendment, the amendment that includes "equal protection" before the law. Although the amendment became effective in 1868, Maryland did not approve it until 1959, when Senator Mathias was in the state legislature and voted for its adoption. As the senator wryly noted, "I am willing to go to the Department of Justice to give Attorney General Meese my original intent of the 14th Amendment. There can be no doubt that it is going to be an original one."[5]

While whose intent should be controlling is difficult to discern, this issue has been cleared up somewhat in the years since Mathias wrote his law review article in 1987. Now, so-called "New Originalists" argue for substituting the intent of what a "reasonable person" would understand as the meaning of the words at the time of the Constitution or its amendments, instead of the collective intent of the drafters and/or ratifiers. Curiously, this New Originalism would still not have settled Madison's and Hamilton's disagreement over whether Congress had the authority to create a national bank. Each was looking at the supposed meaning of the words at the time the Constitution was created. The Supreme Court resolved the issue in 1819 in *McCulloch v. Maryland*, which held that Congress had powers implied by the Constitution's "necessary and proper" clause.

Senator Mathias also questioned whether the founders or ratifiers even wanted original intent to govern how the Constitution would be interpreted—was it the original intent that "original intent" should rule forever? There's no clear answer. A compelling piece of evidence is that perhaps the most authoritative account of the Constitutional convention is found in James Madison's notes in 1787. But the notes of the man often called the "father of the Constitution" were not made public until 1840, four years after his death. So for the first 50 years or so of the Constitution's existence, Supreme Court decisions were reached without benefit of this important source of the document's intent.

Perhaps the most vexing issue Senator Mathias raised about originalism is why we should be bound by an earlier generation's understanding of the Constitution. Why isn't our understanding of this organic document sufficient? If governmental power derives from the consent of the governed, should not our consent rest on our understanding? As Thomas Jefferson wrote in a letter to James Madison, "the earth belongs to the living, and not to the dead … one generation is to another as one independent nation is to another."[6]

As Senator Mathias put it, "[a]rbitrarily fixing the meaning to the intent of the founders robs modern America of the power to consent. It dismisses two centuries of our national dialogue with the Constitution." Indeed, it ignores the significant growth in our understanding of what constitutes this "new order." Mathias makes an essential point in demonstrating the importance of our learned experience in citing former justice Thurgood Marshall's comment: "When the Founders used [the phrase 'We the People'] in 1787 they did not have in mind a majority of American citizens."[7] Left out, of course, were African Americans, Native Americans, women and even property-less White males. To paraphrase the philosopher George Santayana, ignoring what we learn from our history condemns us to repeat it.

Senator Mathias did not simply criticize but offered an alternative to originalism, which he called "ordered liberty," a term likely first used by the Supreme Court in *Palko v. Connecticut* (1937). In that case, the Supreme Court held that certain fundamental rights were so essential to our ordered liberty that the rights were incorporated into the due process clause of the 14th Amendment and applicable to the states. Ordered liberty has appeared in other important cases since that time. For example, *Griswold v. Connecticut* (1965) established a right to privacy for married couples to use contraceptives; *Obergefell v. Hodges* (2015) provided a constitutional right for same-sex couples to marry.

Ordered liberty allows the Constitution's meaning to grow and evolve, rather than, as Senator Mathias stated, "spring full blown like Athena out of the head of Zeus." Instead, it examines the words of the Constitution and where there is ambiguity, then, like originalism, ordered liberty looks to original understanding, but it does not stop there.[8]

Ordered liberty goes beyond originalism by also examining caselaw precedent, tradition, history, and our current understanding of the circumstances we confront. Indeed, this search is anticipated by the Constitution's Ninth Amendment: "[t]he enumeration in the Constitution, of certain rights, shall not be construed to deny or disparage others retained by the people." In essence, ordered liberty requires a conversation of sorts, a reasoned inquiry into the concepts of liberty and equality promised in our founding documents.

Senator Mathias recognized that if we don't use all our tools to reveal the Constitution's meaning—our historical experience, precedent, reason, tradition, underlying Constitutional principles—we cripple our understanding of how this document relates to our current world, with troubling consequences.

The strict application of originalism would very likely undermine many well-established areas of the law. Under originalism, the Supreme Court would not have reached its decision desegregating schools in *Brown v. Board of Education* (1954) because the "separate but equal" doctrine would not have been unconstitutional. Segregated schools were lawful in many states at the time of the 14th Amendment's enactment in 1868, including several Northern states. Indeed, even Congress allowed segregated schools in our nation's capital.[9]

Moreover, constitutional protections for women established in a line of Supreme Court cases in the 1970s would be in jeopardy, since the "equal protection" clause of the 14th Amendment clearly had no application to women or sex discrimination when it was adopted in the 19th century. Laws forbidding interracial marriage could once again be legal and therefore disallow marriages between Blacks and Whites. Laws forbidding same sex marriage could be again legal. As would laws that disallow, as Connecticut had, the use of birth control methods even between married couples.

Like so many things today, the debate over how to interpret the Constitution is mired in partisan politics. Proponents of originalism argue that it's a neutral method that takes politics out of interpreting the Constitution. But originalism is supported much more by Republicans and conservatives than Democrats and progressives. Indeed, many on the political left see originalism as a Trojan horse designed to gut the liberal decisions of the Warren and Burger courts.

There are strong arguments against originalism. Still, it may seem a bit odd that Senator Mathias, a lifelong Republican, should so strongly oppose it. So why not support originalism as most of his fellow Republicans did, or why stay in a political party at such variance with him on such an essential issue?

When he was first elected to Congress in 1960, then–Congressman Mathias joined the liberal or moderate wing of the Republicans and joined with Northern and Western Democrats to pass important civil rights legislation. But the Republican party was changing. By the time Mathias was elected to the Senate in 1968, President Nixon was employing his "Southern Strategy" to use race as a wedge issue to attract Southern Democrats to the Republican Party. Senator Mathias opposed the Southern Strategy, and he also voted against, and helped defeat, two of President Nixon's Supreme Court appointments. Later, he opposed many of President

Reagan's proposals. There was payback from the growing, harder-edged wing of the party: Mathias was due to ascend to the chair of the Senate Judiciary Committee in 1981, but conservative party leaders blocked him. Even in his home state, Mathias received criticism from his party—one delegate to the state Republican convention called him a "liberal swine."

So why did Senator Mathias stay in a party he was increasingly estranged from? One answer is tradition. Mathias was proud that when his great-grandfather ran as a Maryland Senate candidate in 1860, he was on the same ticket as Abraham Lincoln. His family's roots go back to the Republican Party's founding.

But there is a deeper reason. When asked why he remained a Republican, he would answer by telling a story about a farmer and his wife who rode to church every Sunday in their wagon. Over time, the distance between them on the buggy board grew larger. One Sunday, the farmer's wife asked him why he had moved so far away, to which the farmer replied, "Are you sure it is me that has moved?"

Like the farmer, Senator Mathias believed that it was his party that had moved from its laudable traditions, not him. He believed he remained true to the same conservative ideals the Republican Party had at its founding in the mid–19th century. Mathias viewed interpreting the Constitution as President Lincoln had seen it, as a document that required our understanding of it to grow and evolve. The Constitution did not proclaim a static doctrine but was animated by evolving concepts of liberty and equality.

To see this more clearly, consider President Lincoln's position on slavery and emancipation. When Lincoln ran for President in 1860, he accepted the Constitutional compromise that allowed slavery. Although he personally opposed slavery and opposed expanding it to new territories, he saw it as vital to the agreement that held the country together. For Lincoln, slavery was morally wrong but a politically necessary part of the Constitution.[10]

His election to the White House in 1860 caused Southern states, some of which did not even include him on the ballot, to bolt from the Union. Still, as late as the summer of 1862, Lincoln supported a restoration of the Union that included allowing Southern states to rejoin with slavery intact. In response to a public letter from Horace Greeley, the editor of *The New York Tribune*, Lincoln wrote that preserving the Union was his principal concern, not emancipating slaves.

Lincoln's position would change, of course. He issued the Emancipation Proclamation on January 1, 1863. And although he had previously doubted whether he could preserve the Constitution and the Union without slavery, the Emancipation Proclamation freed the slaves in the states that were in rebellion. Lincoln came to recognize that for reasons of morality and military necessity, the Union under the Constitution would need to be reconstituted. Indeed, more than 200,000 African Americans would serve in the Union army.

As Garry Wills pointed out in his book on the Gettysburg Address, Lincoln recast the Civil War to preserve freedom and equality as necessary for restoring the Union.[11] Constitutional interpretation would now look to the Declaration of Independence with its grand pronouncement of equality and inalienable rights. It was "a new birth of freedom." If liberty and equality were the true goals of the nation, then slavery would have to go.

This short, powerful address was a major transformation in the purpose of the Civil War and, ultimately, the Constitution. Those who gave their lives at Gettysburg and the many other Civil War battlefields died in the name of creating a new order. Lincoln learned from his lived experience, evolving and growing in his understanding of the Civil War's purpose. He used that experience to interpret the Constitution and what it said about slavery, freedom and equality. The more than 600,000 who died on the battlefields would help provide a new meaning for the Constitution.

Like President Lincoln, Senator Mathias saw the need for the evolution and growth in our understanding of the Constitution and our relation to it. Mathias would in many ways pick up where President Lincoln left off, working as a leader in the adoption of the 1964 Civil Rights Act and

Returning the (GOP) elephant (Tom Flannery, *The Baltimore Sun*, December 26, 1976. Baltimore Sun Media. All Rights Reserved).

the 1965 Voting Rights Act. He continued the fight for an America motivated, as Lincoln would say in the Second Inaugural, "with malice toward
none with charity for all with firmness in the right as God gives us to see
the right let us strive on to finish the work...." Senator Mathias' work on
these and other issues emerged from his broader vision of living in a country that was supported by a Constitution that can and should speak to liberty, equality and the "better angels of our nature."

Notes

1. Charles M. Mathias, Jr., *Ordered Liberty: The Original Intent of the Constitution*, 47 Md. L. Rev. 174 (1987).
2. R. Bork, *The Constitution, Original Intent and Economic Rights*, 23 San Diego L. Rev. 23 (1986) (address before the University of San Diego Law School).
3. E. Chemerinsky, *Worse Than Nothing: The Dangerous Fallacy of Originalism*, Yale University Press, 2022.
4. Address by Attorney General Edwin Meese, III, before the D.C. Chapter of the Fed-eralist Society, Lawyers Division, in Washington, D.C. (November 15, 1985) (available at the Md. L. Rev.); Speech by Justice Antonin Scalia before the attorney general's Conference on Economic Liberties in Washington, D.C. (June 14, 1986) (available at the Md. L. Rev.).
5. Charles M. Mathias Jr., *Response to Comments*, 47 Md. L. Rev. 234 (1987).
6. D. Strauss, *The Living Constitution*, Oxford University Press, 2010.
7. T. Marshall, remarks at the annual seminar of the San Francisco Patent and Trade-mark Law Association in Maui, Hawaii (May 6, 1987) (available at the Md. L. Rev.).
8. See, e.g., D. Strauss, *The Living Constitution*, Oxford University Press, 2010; M. Lun-der, *The Concept of Ordered Liberty and the Common-Law Due-Process Tradition*, Lexing-ton, 2021.
9. D. Strauss, *The Living Constitution*, Oxford University Press, 2010.
10. N. Feldman, *The Broken Constitution: Lincoln, Slavery and the Refounding of Amer-ica*, Farrar, Straus and Giroux ebook, 2021.
11. G. Wills, *Lincoln at Gettysburg: The Words That Remade America*, Simon & Schus-ter, 1992.

III. Bipartisan Spirit

Reaching Across the Aisle
on South Africa Sanctions

Frederic B. Hill

Room 419 of the Dirksen Senate Office Building was jam-packed on July 23, 1986. Reporters, photographers and television technicians filled all available seats and space for the press. All spectators' chairs were occupied, and many people waited in the hall outside.

In a sure sign of the critical nature of the subject, and the import of the primary witness, almost all 17 Republican and Democratic members of the committee were present.

The subject: Senate bill 99–440 titled "The Comprehensive Anti-Apartheid Act of 1986." The main witness: George Shultz, Secretary of State of the Reagan administration.

For months, the administration had pressed its policy of "constructive engagement" against the besieged South African regime, in which five million Whites ruled over 24 million Blacks. Anti-government demonstrations and the government's crackdown had led to hundreds of deaths for months. While critical of the regime's policies and repression, the Reagan administration's tame sanctions were harshly condemned by most Democrats in Congress and many Republicans.[1]

The Democratic leadership in both the Senate and the House now had growing support for much tougher measures from many Republicans. And it was evident during that July 1986 hearing.

Spectators and reporters witnessed one of the most climactic, tension-filled hearings of the entire Reagan presidency—one surpassed in passion by perhaps only the Iran-contra scandal. The hearing lasted four hours, and, unlike most hearings, most senators on the committee stayed in the room.

The testy hearing reached a climax in a long shouting match between Shultz and Senator Joseph R. Biden. Tension had been building slowly in early parts of the hearing as members made opening statements and Shultz outlined the administration's position—highlighted the previous day by a statement from President Reagan defending his limited sanctions and cautious approach to the South African regime.

Shultz said that the United States must do "all that we can to reverse the forces that are leading to this deepening tragedy there." But while conceding that the situation was getting worse, he argued that the United States could only do so much. "The fate of South Africa is in their hands."

Soon afterward, when it was his turn to speak, Senator Biden lambasted the administration's policy. His voice rising, Biden said the Reagan administration's policy was "nauseating." It was slapping the regime on the wrist while hundreds of people were dying at the hands of "a repulsive, repugnant regime."

"What disturbs me more than the policy that you call a policy is the rationale for the policy," Biden stormed. "[You say,] we must not aim to impose ourselves, our solutions, our favorites in South Africa."

"Damn it, we have favorites in South Africa. The favorites in South Africa are the majority people of South Africa … and they are being crushed. I am ashamed at the lack of a moral backbone [in U.S. policy]," the Delaware senator snapped.

Bristling, Shultz quickly replied, "I resent that deeply because there is tremendous moral backbone on a bipartisan basis."

Biden: "There is no bipartisan basis."

Shultz: "There is. I doubt very much if there is any real objective disagreement if there's going to be any kind of change like you want. The question is what can we do to make that happen."

Tempers calmed after several minutes. Shultz displayed remarkable poise and even helped lower the temperature in the room when he said, "you know, just because I'm secretary of state, you can't kick me around. I'm a taxpayer."

Tension also eased when the committee chairman, Richard Lugar (R–IN), turned to the next speaker in the rotation from one party member to another—a popular and widely respected Republican senator, Charles "Mac" Mathias, Jr., of Maryland.

Displaying his characteristically wry grin, Mathias paused for a moment, surveyed the room and said, "I'd like to make a statement if I can dig myself out from under the lava." The room erupted in laughter.

Unseen moments before, as Biden was roaring at Shultz, Mathias had already taken a step to ease tensions. He had slipped a brief note to the Delaware senator. As the 46th president recalled during his 2010 eulogy of Senator Mathias, the note said, "Calm down, big fella, calm down."

The hearing continued well into the afternoon, highlighted by equally

Secretary of State George Shultz testifying before the Senate Foreign Relations Committee on South Africa sanctions, July 23, 1986—appealing to the Senate not to bind Reagan administration to "a straitjacket of rigid legislation." Chester Crocker, Assistant Secretary of State for African Affairs, is at right (AP Photo/J. Scott Applewhite).

tough criticism of the administration's "constructive engagement" by both Republican senators such as Mathias and Nancy Kassebaum of Kansas and many Democrats, Mathias' Maryland colleague Paul Sarbanes, Ted Kennedy and John Kerry of Massachusetts, and Christopher Dodd of Connecticut.

Biden left the hearing room not long after his statement for another committee hearing. Perhaps taking heed of Senator Mathias' gentle suggestion, Biden sent a note back to the committee which chairman Lugar interrupted the hearing to convey: "Senator Biden has asked to say that he had to leave for [another committee hearing]. He wanted to leave his respects with you, [Mr. Shultz], and say that the exchange was a heated one, but he felt it was one with good humor and in good spirit."

The room erupted in laughter once again.

One senator was heard to ruminate that "it's been a long day." But, smiling, the ever-poised secretary of state said, "Oh, no, this is my day to be here, and I'll be here all day if you want."[2]

The aftermath of the long hearing was inconclusive at first. The committee, with a slight 9–8 GOP majority, narrowly rejected two sweeping Democratic sanctions bills that would have placed virtually a total trade embargo on South Africa; similar bills had been passed overwhelmingly by the Democratic-led House.

* * *

Yet, a week later, support formed behind changes authored by Senator Mathias and Senator Daniel Evans, a moderate Republican from Washington, that deleted a few of the more extreme Democratic measures (e.g., closing the U.S. embassy in South Africa)—yet were tougher than those proposed by their own chairman, Senator Lugar.

The Mathias-Evans amendments, which this writer and (current) Senator Chris Van Hollen, who comprised Senator Mathias' staff on foreign policy, worked on with Senator Evans' staff, would bar any new U.S. investment in South Africa, forbid bank loans to its government, ban imports of South African steel, uranium ore and coal, and ban imports of food and agricultural products unless there was quick progress toward ending apartheid.

"It seems to me we have to touch more than the South African government," Senator Mathias said at the time. The United States "must touch the White power structure," show the Black majority the United States is "prepared to do more than make speeches," and "reach allies who look to us for leadership."

Despite opposition from a few Republicans, the legislation—with the Mathias-Evans amendments—was approved by the committee, at first narrowly, but then on August 1 by a vote of 15–2. On the Senate floor, it was approved on August 15, with a few nominal changes, by an overwhelming vote of 84–14.[3]

Despite such a stunning shot across the bow of a president, Reagan vetoed the bill on September 26. He defended his policy against apartheid, arguing that the sanctions amounted to "economic warfare," would hurt the Black majority and create even more turmoil.

Reagan offered to impose several of the sanctions in the bill by executive order; he said he would meet with Bishop Desmond Tutu, a popular and respected leader of the Black majority. He made dozens of phone calls.

But, on October 2, his veto was overturned by a vote of 78–21—12 votes more than the two-thirds margin needed to do so. It was one of the extremely rare instances in American history when a presidential veto of a major foreign policy issue had been overturned. (The 1973 override of Nixon's veto of the War Powers Act [75–18] was another signal act of strong Congressional bipartisanship.)

The most startling outcome was the scale of Reagan's defeat. At the very height of his popularity, a year before the troubling Iran-contra scandal broke and nearly paralyzed his last year in office, 31 Republicans joined the minority's 47 Democrats to overturn the veto.

Looking back today, the remarkable bipartisanship of that vote on a critical issue of national importance, and featuring full-throated opposition to a hugely popular president by 31 of his 53 GOP senators, is hard to fathom.[4]

But it is clear that three decades ago, members of both parties, notably Republicans, placed a far higher value on the rule of law and what was best for the national interest, well above loyalty to a polarizing political figure like Donald Trump. Many of the senators who voted to overturn Reagan's veto were rock-ribbed conservatives from Midwestern farm states.

One of the Republicans who voted to overturn the veto was a first-term senator from Kentucky, Mitch McConnell. He said, "I think [Reagan] is ill-advised. I think he is wrong. We have waited long enough for him to come on board."

* * *

Senator Mathias' role in enacting one of the most significant foreign policy measures of the later 20th century was underlined in Joseph Biden's moving tribute to the senator during the memorial service for Senator Mathias at the National Cathedral on February 6, 2010.

Their offices close to each other in the Senate Russell Office Building, Biden recalled how he had stopped by to see Senator Mathias after the South Africa hearing ended and dodged the senator's welcoming Chesapeake Bay retriever. Biden said, "Mac had a little table in front of his desk with a tea set on it. He got up from behind his desk in that rumpled suit. I was still fuming [about the hearing]. He walked around and poured a cup of tea and said, 'Sit down, Joe. This will help you.'"

Continuing his eulogy, Biden then noted, referring to passage of the sanctions bill, "He ended up leading the fight that succeeded in getting the very objective accomplished that I cared so deeply about."

Then, mentioning several respected senators, including J. William Fulbright, Mike Mansfield, John Sherman Cooper, Clifford Case and Mathias, Biden said, "These men formed the intellectual and moral compass of the United States. They came from different parties and different backgrounds, but they shared one thing in common. They believed in basic human decency, gender and racial equality. They belonged to a political party—but they were patriots first."

* * *

Mac Mathias was indeed one of the first Republican senators to stand four-square in favor of a tougher policy against the government of South Africa and its system of apartheid.

Not long after House Democrats had stepped up their campaign to punish the government, an effort that went back to the mid–1970s, the soft-spoken senator delivered a no-nonsense speech on the Senate floor on June 11, 1985. Acknowledging that he was not a big fan of sanctions, he said the South African government had continued to promise change but never followed through—resulting in an escalation in frustration and violence.

"They delude themselves that they can continue to live in a dream-world where one-tenth of the population exercises all the power and enjoys all the profits." He called for an escalating series of sanctions that would make clear to the White Afrikaners that they could "no longer lay claim to being part of the West and the free world."

As political maneuvers intensified in 1985 and 1986, Mathias and two Republican colleagues, Evans and Kassebaum, played a pivotal role in steering a pragmatic course between sweeping sanctions pushed by Democratic leaders such as Kennedy, Biden and Dodd and GOP leaders such as Lugar and Majority Leader Bob Dole, who initially were opposed to a tough sanctions bill.

One key move pushed by Senator Mathias was to convince the Democrats to drop some severe provisions—such as a demand to close the U.S. embassy in South Africa. The United States, he argued, should want to keep a full-fledged diplomatic and intelligence presence—not only to keep tabs on what was happening in the country but also to retain contact with Black majority leaders who might eventually come to power.

On the day of the Senate's overturn of President Reagan's veto, Senator Mathias gave voice to his main argument in a speech on the Senate floor—with characteristic vision and understatement.

> With this legislation, we have an opportunity to put together a more coherent, a more active policy, a full-court press by this Administration that has been lacking to date.
>
> Some say we are interfering in another nation's affairs...... I don't agree that it is not our business. We bear a heavy responsibility. As a great nation, as a nation committed to freedom and human rights, it is our business to be concerned with a persistent pattern of repression and inhumanity that threatens to undermine not only one important country but an entire region.

* * *

Stunningly, passage of the Comprehensive Anti-Apartheid Act had a real payoff. Unlike so many sanctions, the virtual shutdown of American relations with South Africa, and a virtual end to economic and military ties, was effective.

International opposition to South Africa's brutal rule, in which only Whites were allowed to vote and the vast majority of people suffered from poverty, malnutrition and disease, had gained strength in the 1960s and

Nelson Mandela and Frederik W. de Klerk at the Grand Hotel, Oslo, Norway, December 9, 1993, on the eve of their joint award of the Nobel Peace Prize (AP Photo/Jon Eeg).

'70s. Growing internal resistance by different Black, mixed race and Asian (Indian) people began to mount and was matched by outside condemnation and limited reforms.

But the largest cracks in the apartheid system came in the 1980s, marked by rising tensions within the country, global pressures, including stiff American and European sanctions, and a military setback in neighboring Angola.

Replacement in 1989 of the hardline president, P.W. Botha, by a more moderate leader, Frederik W. de Klerk, led to discussions on the release of Nelson Mandela, the leader of the main opposition, the African National Congress. Mandela's release from prison on the notorious Robben Island where he had been held for 27 years was a main demand of virtually every sanction against the government—including the 1986 Act.

Head-spinning events began when de Klerk delivered a dramatic address to parliament on February 2, 1990, in which he recognized South Africa's deep-seated ills and promised radical change. That came rapidly—first with Mandela's release nine days later and a series of negotiations between the government and the ANC leaders to seek a new constitution and bring about a peaceful transition to majority rule.[5]

The negotiations, held in the midst of rising violence within both camps, culminated in a referendum in 1992 and an agreement at the end of 1993—for which Mandela and de Klerk were awarded the Nobel Peace Prize. The first free elections were held in April 1994, and Mandela was sworn in as president on May 10 of that year.

* * *

Many factors led to the dramatic decision by the White minority regime to turn over power to the Black majority in 1990–91. The international order was breaking up with the end of the Cold War, starting with the fall of the Berlin Wall in 1989 and the collapse of the Soviet Union in 1991. The collapse weakened pro–Soviet forces in neighboring countries such as Angola and Mozambique. The heightened influence of the United States, now considered the sole superpower, for a brief period, at least, also stood out.

Senator Mathias' role in the enactment of the anti-apartheid act was one of many instances of his principled independence, his readiness to stand up for civil rights, the rule of law, campaign finance reform, environmental measures and health care—often in defiance of his party. As noted in other essays, Mathias was one of several Republican members of the House of Representatives to back what became the Civil Rights Act of 1964 *after* the failure of assassinated President John F. Kennedy's efforts and before Lyndon Johnson threw his weight behind it.

An outspoken critic of the Vietnam war, Mathias was one of the very first Republican senators to criticize Richard M. Nixon as the Watergate scandal unfolded in 1973 and 1974—the first GOP member of the Judiciary Committee to join Democrats in backing an investigation of the president's actions.

Perhaps the most enduring legacy of the South Africa sanctions period and set of issues today was the remarkable bipartisanship at work in the 99th Congress (1985–87) and for all too short a period thereafter.

Unlike the vast majority of GOP members of Congress today, in thrall to a far less popular former president than Reagan, one who accomplished very little in four years, largely ignored a deadly pandemic and sought to overturn a legitimate election, these Republicans voted their conscience and what they deemed the national interest.

Recall Joseph Biden's remarks at the memorial service for Senator Mathias at the National Cathedral:

> You have read a lot since his death about how he reached across the aisle. I thought of him as never even recognizing there was an aisle.
>
> It was who he was. There was no artificial divide. There was only principle. He approached every issue with his principles firm, but with his mind open. To

Mac, right or wrong, you were not defined by whether you had a D or an R after your name. You were defined by what was in your heart.

I would only add "and what is in the national interest."

Notes

1. https://www.nytimes.com/1986/07/23/world/transcript-of-talk-by-reagan-on-south-africa-and-apartheid.html.

2. https://www.c-span.org/video/?150206-1/south-africa-policies.

3. https://www.nytimes.com/1986/08/02/world/senate-unit-votes-strict-sanctions-on-south-africa.html.

4. https://www.nytimes.com/1986/10/03/politics/senate-78-to-21-overrides-reagans-veto-and-imposes-sanctions-on.html.

5. https://omalley.nelsonmandela.org/index.php/site/q/03lv02039/04lv02103/05lv02104/06lv02105.html.

Two Senators, Two Parties, One Goal

Judith Davison Keenan

From the time Paul S. Sarbanes entered the Senate in January 1977 until Charles "Mac" Mathias retired in January 1987, they worked together to advance the state of Maryland's interests. At first, they seemed an odd couple. They belonged to opposing political parties. They came from different generations. They grew up in vastly different regions of their oddly-shaped state, and perhaps most significantly, their family backgrounds reflected two profoundly different versions of the American experience. Any or all of these could have impeded a harmonious and effective working relationship. None ever did. Barbara Mikulski, who ran unsuccessfully against Mac Mathias in 1974 and a dozen years later became his successor, called their joint efforts "a great expression of Team Maryland!"

Fifty or so years ago the political divide meant something very different from what it means today. When Mac Mathias entered the Senate in 1969, he joined a bloc of Republican senators—liberals and moderates—who formed their party's dominant voice: Minority Leader Hugh Scott of Pennsylvania, Jacob Javits of New York, Clifford Case of New Jersey, Chuck Percy of Illinois, Howard Baker of Tennessee, Edward Brooke of Massachusetts and others. At that time split Democratic-Republican Senate delegations were common; there were 21 among the 50 states. The raging debate over the war in Vietnam was not a party-line issue. Notwithstanding hysterical attacks on the proposed Panama Canal treaties, in 1978, 16 of the 41 Republicans voted to ratify them. Even California's Senator Sam Hayakawa famously declared "we stole it fair and square."

Retirement and electoral defeat diminished the liberal GOP bloc over the course of the '70s, and with the Reagan election in 1980, when 12 Democratic seats turned Republican, Mac Mathias' party moved sharply to the right. Not Mathias: he stayed where he had always been. Inevitably, he was increasingly estranged from his party. When party conservatives accused him of being a liberal, he told them that, on the contrary, he was a conservative—he was conserving the Constitution.

Would the Mathias-Sarbanes working relationship have suffered if Mathias had followed his party's lead? Given their shared respect for the institution in which they were serving, it would probably have remained correct in public but a lot less congenial in private. At the staff level it would have wreaked havoc.

Although the two senators were just a decade apart in age, World War II created a generational divide. Mathias enlisted in the Navy in 1942, at the age of 20, and served four years in the Pacific theater and then in the occupation of Japan. Sarbanes was 12 years old when the war ended. He belonged to that in-between generation referred to disparagingly (and unfairly) as the Silent Generation: too young to serve in the world war, too old to qualify as a Baby Boomer or serve in Vietnam. But their varying experience of the war—close-up for Senator Mathias, child's-eye for Senator Sarbanes—did not leave them with differing perspectives on critical issues such as civil rights and the Vietnam War that were then facing the country.

Nor did the formative experience of growing up in vastly different regions of their state. Roughly 250 miles separate Frederick and Salisbury, but before the opening of the Bay Bridge in 1952, they might have been on different planets; it was easier to go from Salisbury to Philadelphia than to Baltimore. Mac Mathias' hometown of Frederick lies northwest of both Baltimore and the District of Columbia in what was mainly farmland country; a busy town, Frederick was a gateway to the west. Salisbury lies on Maryland's Eastern Shore, the sliver of the state east of the Chesapeake Bay that stretches north to south from Delaware to Virginia. Until the Civil War it was tobacco plantation country (both Frederick Douglass and Harriet Tubman were born enslaved on Eastern Shore plantations). In 1960, as a newly married law school graduate, Paul Sarbanes made Baltimore his hometown. When he was elected to the House of Representatives in 1970, it was the sixth largest city in the country, a major port and industrial center with a population soon to be majority Black. Frederick was still largely the small city in which Mac Mathias had grown up and always considered home.

The most striking distinction between Mac Mathias and Paul Sarbanes lay in their family backgrounds. Mac's family was long established in Frederick and also in Republican state politics. Both his great-grandfather and his grandfather had served in the Maryland legislature, and while his father never held public office, when Mac was a child his father took him to the White House to meet presidents Coolidge and Hoover.

Paul Sarbanes was a first-generation American, the son of Greek immigrants who had come from villages in Laconia—Sparta in ancient Greece. They had little education and spoke little English; Paul Sarbanes spoke Greek until he went to school. They settled on the Eastern Shore because relatives were already living there. Salisbury became their hometown because it had a place to open a restaurant. Like Greek restaurants everywhere, it was a family affair. Paul Sarbanes worked in the restaurant after school.

Further, Paul Sarbanes was an outlier. Mac Mathias won his Senate seat in 1968 by defeating the incumbent, Daniel Brewster, an old friend and law school roommate. Paul Sarbanes won his Senate seat in 1976 by defeating J. Glenn Beall, who six years earlier had defeated Joseph Tydings, who in turn had defeated Beall's father. Earlier, Tydings' step-father, Millard Tydings, had served four terms. The Sarbanes name was something entirely new in Maryland politics.

None of these distinctions—party, generation, hometown, family— affected the two senators' collaborative efforts on behalf of their state. The underpinning of their work together was the principle President Grover Cleveland had set out nearly a century earlier: "Public Office is a Public Trust." Public office was never about self-aggrandizement, whether financial, social or psychological. Paul Sarbanes and Mac Mathias did not hold office to advance an ideology or a party; they were there to serve the people of Maryland and the nation.

"Team Maryland" applied to their joint efforts on behalf of their state, but as two of 100 Senate legislators dealing with national issues, each went his own way. There were some notable differences. They caucused with their respective parties. They sat on different committees. Mathias' assignments included Judiciary and Appropriations, then Foreign Relations and Rules (which he chaired), plus the Joint Committees on Printing and the Library. Paul Sarbanes served on the Foreign Relations and Banking Committees for 30 years, briefly chairing Banking when, in mid–2001, Vermont senator Jim Jeffords left the Republican Party and the Democrats took the majority.

Perhaps the most signal achievement of Senator Sarbanes' career came with passage of the Sarbanes/Oxley legislation in 2002. After numerous financial scandals such as the Enron and WorldCom cases, Sarbanes/ Oxley established much tougher standards and penalties to protect investors against fraudulent financial practices in the corporate world.

While Mathias and Sarbanes saw eye to eye on most domestic matters, especially civil rights, voting rights, aid to cities and anti-poverty programs, they had their differences—mostly on macroeconomic issues and foreign policy.

They differed on deregulation of gas and oil production and prices, a fiery issue following the oil embargo and rising fuel prices in the 1970s. In an effort to spur domestic production of fossil fuels, the 1978 Natural Gas Policy Act opened the door to deregulation. Sarbanes fought it vigorously; Mathias supported it. Mathias supported the AWACS sale to Saudi Arabia while Sarbanes opposed it, a vote reflecting their differing perspectives on Israel and the Middle East. When after a year's delay Ed Meese was confirmed 63–31 to be President Reagan's attorney general, the two Maryland senators were again on opposing sides.

Despite disagreement on one provision of the Anti-Apartheid Act against South Africa in 1986—whether South African Airways flights should be barred from the United States, which Sarbanes backed but Mathias opposed—they agreed on the overall sanctions against the brutal White minority regime. Thirty-one Republicans joined all 47 Democrats to overturn Reagan's veto of the bill by a vote of 78–21, one of the most remarkable examples of bipartisanship in recent history.

* * *

The voting analyses published annually by two very different organizations, the American Conservative Union and Americans for Democratic Action, underline a striking consistency in the voting records of the two senators.

The ACU gave both senators very low marks—Mathias a lifetime rating of 11.45, Sarbanes 5.07 percent. Both were given zeroes in 1986, the last year they served together. The ADA does not offer lifetime ratings, but the ADA's annual ratings show them at 75 percent and 90 percent, respectively, in 1977—the first year they served together—and 80 percent and 100 percent in the last.

The two senators had something else in common, wholly unrelated to their voting records and all too rare in the world of politics: a self-deprecating sense of humor. Often Paul Sarbanes would tell his listeners what his mother had said about him to a gathering of Greek American women: "He's been a good boy—*so far.*" Or he might tell them about an inter-parliamentary conference when, as a courtesy to his Greek counterparts, he spoke Greek until they asked him to stop because, they said, "to us, when you speak Greek, you sound like a six-year-old."

But let Mac Mathias have the last word with a story he saw fit to insert in the Congressional Record. It went something like this.

He was on a dock in Stonington, Maine, waiting for the mail boat that would take him to the island of Isle au Haut where his wife's family had a summer residence. A stranger, a Down East native, struck up a conversation.

"I hear you're from Washington, D.C."

"Yes, that's right."

"I bet there are a lot of smart people down there."

"Yes, there are."

"I bet there are a lot of dumb people, too."

"Well, yes."

"And I bet you can hardly tell the difference."

The Long Book of History

Richard L. Berke

When I sat down with Senator Mathias for an interview in 1985 after he announced his retirement from the Senate, I was well aware that he was not your run-of-the-mill member of Congress: Here was a Republican senator who hardly acted like a Republican and, if anything, expressed more fealty to the Democrats.

As I encouraged him to reflect on his career, what I did not know then, nearly 40 years ago, was that Mathias was one of the last of his kind, a Republican who truly respected his peers. Can you imagine the shellacking a Republican senator would get today if he or she dared to praise President Biden with the warmth Mathias showed toward Jimmy Carter? The senator said to me, "I was impressed by his sincerity, his desire to not only be a good president, but a good person."

At the time of that interview, I was a relatively green reporter, learning my way around the Capitol for *The Baltimore Evening Sun*, and Mathias was 63—young for a retiring senator. That was another sign of his confidence, not needing to cling to power. (The average age of a U.S. senator today is 64, and many serve well into their 80s.) Or perhaps he moved on because the role was no longer as fulfilling and he missed his old friends.

Even then I was taken aback when I asked him which colleagues he respected most, and he reflected on a bygone era, citing only senators who were retired or dead.

Four were moderate to liberal Republicans: Jacob Javits of New York, Clifford Case of New Jersey, John Sherman Cooper of Kentucky, and George Aiken of Vermont. And three were Democrats: Majority Leader Mike Mansfield of Montana, J. William Fulbright of Arkansas, and Philip Hart of Michigan.

"These were unusual people," Mathias told me. "This sounds implausible, but it's a fact that I really respect every member of the Senate that I've served with because everyone, regardless of how many I have disagreed

127

with, had some quality that caused their fellow citizens to elect them to the Senate."

Reporters like me appreciated Mathias because he carried himself with dignity and seemed to float above political calculation and TV-camera performances. (Or could it be that he outsmarted all of us, and his secret strategy was to *appear* above it all?) Maybe he could afford to be that way because he was very popular among Maryland voters, though as a Republican in a heavily Democratic state, he always had to be careful to do what it took to get elected. Or maybe his patrician bearing disguised the cunning and ambition he drew on to wrest his seat in the first place from his old friend, Senator Daniel Brewster.

My own attempts at goading him to stray from his calm confidence—and disparage colleagues whom he did not agree with—never worked. And he never seemed fazed by the optics of the company he kept. In the eulogy he gave at Mathias' memorial service in 2010, Vice President Biden spoke of his old friend "marching with Gloria Steinem and Bella Abzug." Can you imagine that image?

I chronicled how the senator was often rebuffed by his own party—because of his independence. There was the GOP state party meeting in Ocean City when he barely won enough votes to attend the party's national convention in Dallas in 1984. Allan C. Levey, the state party chairman (diplomatically), told me then: "There are a lot of people here who feel, philosophically, he's not in line with Ronald Reagan."

While Mathias did go to the convention, he was hardly a commanding presence there, if a presence at all. In fact, the Maryland delegation—given its lack of clout in the GOP—was relegated to among the lousiest seats at the convention and rooms at a hotel in the far-out suburbs, at least 45 minutes away from the arena. One delegate went so far as to tell me that he thought the senator's lack of popularity (not just Maryland's) must have had something to do with the inconvenient accommodations.

Mathias took it all in stride, seemingly not bothered by any bad press. His aides, trying their best to speak up for him, reminded me that he hosted a breakfast as well as a pool party for the Maryland delegates staying out in the hinterlands.

It's hard to imagine a Republican today—or even in those days—who talked as brazenly as Mathias often did about the need to raise taxes to reduce the deficit.

At a town meeting with about 400 constituents at Anne Arundel Community College, he let the audience do much of the talking, and acting like a teacher using extensive background notes, he explained the intricacies of the tax code. But he told me afterward that he was steadfast in his belief about fiscal responsibility, even if it ruffled the Reagan White House:

"I was impressed by the repeated expressions of concern over the deficit. It came up again and again from the first of the evening, and I think that demonstrated it's a matter of real worry to the American people."

Can you imagine even *one* Republican senator in the last decade or more who would have pushed as hard for passage of the Civil Rights Act of 1964—and for the voting rights bills of a year later—as Mathias did, prodding two Democratic administrations to act more decisively on these critical issues? Or a Republican senator leading a path-breaking compromise on sanctions against the apartheid regime of South Africa, as he did in 1985 and 1986? (Mathias led 31 GOP senators in joining all 47 Democrats to overturn Reagan's veto of the legislation—at the height of Reagan's popularity.)

While Mathias would surely be aghast at the Republican Party of today, he was hopeful in our last interview that the party would move toward some moderation from the Reagan years. Presciently, he cited George H.W. Bush as a possible president three years before Bush was elected. He said Bush, or Howard Baker, could potentially bring the party back to its centrist roots "if they reestablish their credentials" as moderates.

"What we're seeing today is another chapter in a long book on history," he told me. "Only someone who has a genuine crystal ball could say when this chapter would end."

But he was not prescient at all about the evolution of his party. As I sat there with Mathias, I had no inkling that he might be the last Republican elected to the Senate from Maryland, perhaps in my lifetime.

Not long after, I had an encounter in the basement of the Senate where I was reminded that Mathias' tranquil demeanor was not the standard. Representative Barbara Mikulski bounded up to me in the Capitol basement and grilled me on why—she had heard—I had remarked to someone that I assumed Governor Harry Hughes was a shoo-in to win the Democratic nomination for Mathias' seat. She made the case, convincingly and aggressively, that she would win. She was right, of course.

It was not the sort of encounter I could have ever imagined with Mathias, who in that last interview remained gracious and upbeat, not sounding too wistful about his isolation as a Republican who did not behave like a Republican.

"It's been exciting, exciting more than lonely," he said. "We've always had a lot to do, very few troops to do it."

Little did either of us know that the troops of Mathias-like Republicans would dwindle to a mere shadow of the party's forebears.

IV. Character

"Meth-I-ess"

Sen. Alan K. Simpson (Ret.)

When I was first elected to the Senate in the 1978 election, Mac Mathias took me under his wing. He had then been in the Senate for almost two terms, and he had known my father, who was a senator in the '60s.

We got along well and enjoyed each other's company, since Mac was so independent, and very wise and witty, and not always voting the straight Republican line. Fair-minded GOP majority leader Bob Dole often asked me as his assistant leader to "keep an eye" on Mac when key votes were coming up.

Dole told me one day during an important committee meeting, "Watch the door, Al. Make sure he doesn't escape just when we might need him for a procedural vote."

I would watch carefully, but somehow, just like that, as if he were paranormal, if I turned for a brief moment, he'd be gone, vanished. We never knew how he did it!

He knew all kinds of hiding places to disappear to in the Senate; he would just quietly slip out before a vote or after he voted. He often went over to the Library of Congress or to the Reading Room of the Folger Shakespeare Library, and he didn't want the pressure of changing his vote, a most serious and awkward decision surely to be avoided.

Mac drove Senator Strom Thurmond to distraction. (The Republican senator from South Carolina had blocked Mathias from assuming the chairmanship of the Judiciary Committee.) Thurmond couldn't quite pronounce his name. With that steep Southern accent, he'd often mutter to me, "This guy 'Meth-I-ess' is not really a Republican, is he?"

Despite political differences, Mac was a most well respected and outstanding member of the Senate. A man of conscience. He was very honest, loyal, and straightforward. He was also a warm, civil human being.

He had a magnificent wry and engaging smile—that he managed to conjure up especially when he was really pissing somebody off!

He gave off impulses of calmness when the rest of us were going bonkers.

He had an amazing grasp of detail—whatever the subject. He was a font of detail, important and not so important, and a lover of trivia and beauty.

I remember one warm spring day when we were walking from the Capitol to our offices, he said to me, "Hey, cowboy, see those trees there? You don't have those hardwoods out there in Wyoming."

"Let me tell you what they are." He'd talk about their origins and life spans and when they're going to bloom or leaf out, and he'd go on in great length about his love affair with trees.

I said, "It's true, Mac, we don't have these kinds of trees. We have mostly cottonwoods, pines, aspens and coniferous Douglas fir. You are showing me oaks, maples, elm, cherry and deciduous trees, and doing a damn good job at that!"

Mac was very down to earth, earthy, in fact. He once shared with me a tattered bundle of songs and ditties he and his mates sang on "off to war ships" going to the Pacific in World War II and they felt they might not make it home. I guess they were songs from Boy Scouts, band camps, athletic events and college. They were full of the sayings of young men

Key members of the Senate Judiciary Committee before vote to confirm Sandra Day O'Connor to the Supreme Court, September 15, 1981. From left are Alan Simpson (R–WY); Robert Dole (R–KS); Patrick Leahy (D–VT); Joseph Biden (D–DE); and Charles McC. Mathias, Jr. (R–MD) (AP Photo/Ira Schwarz).

and boys. I knew them well—another bond of ours. He had them written down, and one day he handed me these yellowed sheets of paper and said, "Al, would you have a nostalgic look at these and please burn these for me?" I did.

Mac had a truly exceptional love of history, of Abe Lincoln in particular, and, of course, of Frederick (Maryland), his hometown. One day, not long after I'd been in the Senate, he sidled up to me in that usually rumpled suit of his and said, "Al, I'd like you to give the Lincoln Day address for me in Frederick. I'd be honored if you could do it because I have a conflict."

I was brand new, and I said, "Are you sure?" He said, "Yes, I've come to know you and I've heard you speak, and I'm sure you'll do just fine, and the folks in Frederick will love you!"

I'll never forget that evening. He was trusting me to give an important address in Frederick, for he loved that city and its role in the Civil War. I was quite touched by his request. I was in his thrall. He was then my chum.

As Shakespeare noted, "What friends thou hast—and their adoption tried, bind them to thy soul with hoops of steel."

In later years he was afflicted with Parkinson's disease, as was my dear father who had served with Mac. I told Mac that Dad contracted the malady at 63 and lived to be 95. Mac had told me, "I feel like a prisoner in my own body." Dad had related the same sensation and emotion, and I told Mac when Dad would speak in public he would often say, "I see you are watching my hand going up this invisible rope and trembling, but don't feel sorry for me, but I feel sorry for myself—because that's my drinking hand—and I'm spilling more than I drink!"

Mac loved that. And I loved Mac.

That says it all for me. He lives on in my heart—always.

"30 miles west of Frederick"

Ann Terry Pincus

Two days after I went to work for Senator Mathias in late July 1983, I got a call from CNN, asking to interview the senator. Who knows what they wanted to interview him about? I certainly don't remember. I was thrilled and rushed to his office to set it up.

"All right," said the senator laconically. The next day, the camera crew entered the senator's office to set up the shot. They asked him to sit in a chair with his vast array of books on shelves in the background instead of sitting behind the desk.

The sound man asked him to do a voice test. I assumed he would say, "testing 1, 2, 3, testing." Instead, his voice boomed out:

> Up from the meadows rich with corn,
> Clear in the cool September morn,
> The clustered spires of Frederick stand
> Green-walled by the hills of Maryland.

I learned later those lines were the beginning of *Barbara Frietchie* by John Greenleaf Whittier. At the time, I remember being flabbergasted. Of course, I hadn't known that the senator always quoted *Barbara Frietchie* when asked to do a voice check, but that first time has stuck with me all these years.

Oddly, after the interview was over, Mathias turned to me and asked, "Well, how did I do?"

I responded rather too candidly, "Well, senator, you need to sit up in the chair rather than slump, and you need to keep your eyes wide open so you don't look half asleep."

I added (for good measure): "And we need to be sure that the camera shoots from above and not directly at your neck." My not-so-subtle point was that his neck and throat areas were not the most prepossessing parts of his anatomy.

I will never forget his response. Of course, he ignored my comment about the camera angle, but noted, "I have a problem with hooded eyes and can't open them any further." Oops.

I did manage to compliment him on his remarks to CNN, so I stayed on the job. Mathias' remarks to the press were always just about perfect. He played it straight with the media, never revealing the whole story but always fair and truthful. The media loved that characteristic.

Speaking of *Barbara Frietchie*'s meadows, the Mathias family owned a farm, Bullskin Farm, near Frederick. One day soon after I began working for the senator, a member of the press called. "Rumor has it that the senator from Maryland has a farm in West Virginia," he snapped at me in a "gotcha" fashion.

"I'll call you back," I responded. Then I ran to the senator's office and asked, "Do you have a farm in West Virginia?"

The senator responded, "The farm is 30 miles west of Frederick. That's all you have to say."

I phoned the press person back, and said, indignantly, "How could you think such a thing? Senator Mathias' farm is just west of Frederick!" Of course, West Virginia is 30 miles west of Frederick, but I didn't stress that point, and the reporter dropped the subject.

Mathias loved his farm. The farmhouse, built in the late 18th century, had a bit of history. General George Washington allegedly spent the night there. The senator never disabused anyone of that notion.

The farm—"30 miles west of Frederick" (Mathias Family).

The senator at his farm (Mathias Family).

The most surprising aspect of the farm were the peacocks that strutted around the area between the barn and the house, displaying their magnificent iridescent tail feathers to one and all, including the senator himself, who expressed great pride in their finery. Poor peahens were nowhere to be found. But the senator was at his most genial at the farm; dressed in a lumberjack shirt and rumpled corduroys, he beamed at all visitors and led tours around his apple trees and meadows.

To state the obvious: Mac Mathias was beloved and admired by the press. He always (or almost always) gave them the straight scoop. He explained the issues, treating both sides of an issue fairly, but seldom revealed his voting intentions unless he was ready.

As I think back to the 1980s—when I worked for Senator Mathias—I recall how different the media then were from today. Newspapers had beat reporters who regularly covered congressional delegations, so there was often intense, daily coverage of politicians such as Senator Mathias and his colleagues. That had pluses—lots of sustained press attention—and minuses—sometimes a little too much attention.

The press sought the senator out when controversial votes came up. Mathias played his cards close to his chest and only occasionally hinted at his position. He was a master at playing the Sphinx but equally brilliant at framing political situations. The press loved his clarity on issues, if not always on his position.

Mathias was a benevolent version of today's Joe Manchin—that is, he was the maverick vote in the GOP caucus. Respected by Republican senators such as Jack Heinz and John Danforth, he was feared by senators such as Strom Thurmond and Jesse Helms, who dreaded the "mischief" he could rain down on the party.

Mac Mathias was secretive. Reading his mind was a daily process his staff engaged in. In addition, he was economical with words, never verbose, seldom loquacious. Although willing to talk to the media most of the time, he had several friendships with members of the press which he kept hidden.

He met "secretly" occasionally with media bigwigs, such as Meg Greenfield, editorial page editor of *The Washington Post*, or Rowland Evans, the syndicated columnist. He kept his friendships—and definitely his social meetings with individual press people during the cocktail hour—to himself.

However, I knew about (or actually helped set up) most of his press contacts, other than the close friendships.

* * *

Mathias didn't mind silences and could sit benignly waiting for a companion or an aide to speak. One day, an assistant to Ted Turner called me and asked if Turner could have a meeting with Mathias to discuss copyright-related issues. Mathias agreed to meet with Turner for a coffee in the Senate Dining Room, and he invited me to come along. It was an uncomfortable encounter. Turner couldn't deal with silences—and Mathias seldom engaged in small talk. Turner refused to bring up the subject he wished to discuss and so silence prevailed. In retrospect, Turner probably wanted Mathias to support legislation benefiting cable, but he never asked any questions. Odd.

Despite his taciturn side, the senator could be emotional. He was one of the main drivers behind the effort to build a memorial to honor soldiers who had served and died in the Vietnam War. At a ceremony dedicated to service members killed in the war—a memorial he worked hard to get approved—Mathias was asked to stand and read the names of 50 soldiers. He cried and cried.

A daredevil at the wheel, Mathias drove like Barney Oldfield when he controlled his elderly blue Chevrolet which sported a small hole in the floor of the back seat. I know about the hole because I often traveled with him across Maryland, with at least one other staffer more senior than I who got the front seat. Chammy, the Mathiases' beloved Chesapeake Bay retriever, traveled in the back seat on other occasions, as my clothes would attest. One night, we were zooming down I-270 at breakneck speed. (I urged the senator to slow down as I had three young children, but he paid no heed. He did laugh, however.) We were returning from a speech he had made in Hancock, and he wanted to get home before midnight. The car began to break down in the middle of the highway, going from 90 mph to zero. We coasted over to the side. Unperturbed, Mathias walked across eight lanes to reach a Maryland visitors center in the pitch dark with traffic coming straight at us. He never even blinked. I nearly collapsed crossing the road. A good example of the Mathias equanimity.

As chairman of the Senate Rules Committee, the senator was in charge of providing Internet usage to all the senators and staff in their offices in 1983 and 1984. He proudly displayed the computer that sat—unused—on his desk in his office. He did manage to provide computers and access to all the Senate, but he never sent even one email on his new computer.

Senator Mathias had a subtle yet wry sense of humor and chuckled rather than guffawed. For example, after the unsettling bombing of the Capitol in November 1983, the senator had metal detectors installed at all the entrances to Senate office buildings and to the Capitol. One day, shortly after they were in use, he called me on the intercom and asked me to handle a problem with the metal detectors at the main entrance to the Russell building. Down I went and found Mrs. Quentin Burdick (wife of the North Dakota senator) banned from entering the building. She was a rather well-endowed matron, and her problem was that her brassiere had triggered the metal detector, and the Capitol police wouldn't allow her to enter. Of course, I assured the guards she was not a security risk. Later the senator asked me about it. It turned out he knew the problem and he gently laughed about it.

Neither biting nor mean, his quick wit surfaced long before I knew him. Way back in 1968, when he was running for the Senate, the candidate—according to his press secretary at the time—stopped at a rural diner, where he was confronted by a grizzled truck driver.

"I know who you are," the truck driver yelled. "And I'm not going to vote for you."

"Heck," responded Mathias amicably, "I didn't expect it to be unanimous."

He could be tough-minded when confronted with unpalatable choices.

He pulled me into a rather unpleasant duty when Bob Dole became majority leader. One of Mathias' housekeeping duties was to chair the Committee on Printing, where the Senate documents and other papers were printed and distributed. Perhaps 50 people worked in that office.

For reasons that baffled and disturbed me, Dole decided to fire many of the staff, and he planned to fill the positions with staunch Republicans. The staff—most of whom had worked there for at least 10 years—were outraged and terrified about losing their livelihood. The senator delegated me to speak to the Printing Committee staff. I listened to heartbreaking tales of family disasters and the costs of family illness. I repeated all these unhappy stories to the senator, who told me, "I am not going to challenge Dole on this. I have to confront him on other issues." And that was that.

The senator had one dedicated detractor in the press: a young reporter for *The Baltimore Sun* decided that the senator was lazy and preferred traveling to anywhere in Europe rather than to the Eastern Shore. The reporter also recognized some of the senator's Epicurean traits: in addition to traveling to Europe, he thoroughly enjoyed European cuisine. But the reporter never was able to illustrate that he possessed other, less appealing traits.

Senator Mathias did take great interest and pleasure in international affairs and American foreign policy and did, as a result, travel frequently and widely—especially to Europe, Asia and the Middle East.

His deep engagement and respect among European leaders led to his election as president of the North Atlantic Assembly, the parliamentary arm of NATO, during his third Senate term. He loved that honor and looked forward to speaking French at various Assembly gatherings. One year, toward the end of his final term in office, Mathias presided over the conference session in Istanbul. I went along with him, and his wife Ann and younger son Rob also attended, coming from Saudi Arabia, where he was working.

By custom, opening remarks were to be delivered in French by the president, in this case Mathias, whose French was perhaps a bit rough. He understood the basics but couldn't get the Maryland twang out of his delivery.

As he slowly and deliberately began his welcome to the conference, commenting, *"Je suis tres heureux d'etre ici...,"* listening became painful, even for those of us whose French speaking or accent did not match de Gaulle's. He was unperturbed and carried on, despite smiles from the audience.

Unfortunately (for me) I worked for the senator during his final years in the Senate. Of course, I had no idea he was considering retiring—after all, he was only 63! He did tell me, though, "Ann, I am not going to stay here until the day I die; I want to leave before everyone says I ought to go." He noted about a political career: "Every Member of Congress should have a job they can go back to, so that they can vote their conscience, and not fear losing their income."

In the six months before he announced his retirement, the staff sat around wondering what his plans were. He wasn't out raising money, and he had irritated AIPAC, the Israeli lobbying arm, but he occasionally appeared to have the old fire in his belly.

When he called me into his office and revealed he was not going to run again, I was shocked. "I can't believe you didn't realize I was going to quit," he said. But I just didn't believe it because I didn't want to believe it.

Of course, the senator had a photo taken with each of the staff members. We all paraded into his office, shook hands and the camera flashed.

He wrote personal notes to each of the staff. To me he wrote, "To Ann, who made the sunset glow."

It was a great time.

Just a Glass of Sherry Before Lunch

Stuart S. Janney, III

By the mid–1970s, Mac Mathias was recognized as the leading voice for environmental protection of the Chesapeake Bay. The University of Maryland biology lab was moving to a new building in Solomon's Island and its director Gene Cronin, often referred to as "the Admiral of the Chesapeake," had been a great help to the senator.

Senator Mathias was asked to be the keynote speaker and I was told to prepare a major address on the Bay and the environment. I did and it was many pages long. To this day I think it was quite good.

As we left Washington for the drive to Solomon's Island, the weather was deteriorating. It was with some dismay that we arrived at the new center to find folding chairs in great numbers set up on an exposed piece of ground at the edge of the Bay.

You could feel the temperature dropping and the wind increasing. A glance at the agenda suggested a long ceremony. Officials from the administration of Marvin Mandel, legislative leaders, county officials and the University of Maryland folks all had speaking roles—and speak they did. It seemingly never occurred to any of them to omit a single line. People were literally shaking with cold when Senator Mathias was introduced.

Mathias stood up, looked around, took his speech out of its folder, held it up and slowly thumbed its many pages. He informed the audience that there would be other opportunities for him to deliver remarks on the future of the Bay. He then folded the speech and put it in his breast pocket to thunderous applause and cheers as he descended from the platform.

He made his way over to me to say that he was very sorry to have done that to my wonderful speech, but given the circumstances this was the best way to ensure that his remarks would be well received. Of all the important people on the agenda that day he was the only one aware of his environment and able to think on his feet.

In many ways, this unusual incident, this non-speech reflects—as much as more momentous legislative achievements—the very special, singular character of Charles McCurdy Mathias, Jr., and his remarkable career. As much as I was pained by the non-use of my research and prose, it demonstrated Mac Mathias' shrewd political sense, intelligence and a certain modesty that allowed this native of Frederick, Maryland, to stand out as an effective, memorable and highly respected senator during three decades in political life. And all that as a Lincoln-like Republican in a heavily Democratic state who never lost an election.

I worked for Mathias when he was in his late 40s and early 50s. I saw a man of great intelligence, certainly ambitious but presented in a very attractive form. Picture a duck serenely gliding across the pond, leaving no evidence of the vigorous paddling which may be occurring just below the surface. He had a measured approach to most aspects of life and was prone to step back and look at the big picture, often to pursue facets of an issue that struck his intellectual curiosity. If there was anyone in the larger

The Sphinx cartoon. Other Maryland politicos trying to figure out if Mathias is running for office (Tom Flannery, *The Baltimore Sun*, September 25, 1985. Baltimore Sun Media. All Rights Reserved).

Senate community of his colleagues and staff that didn't like Mac, I was never aware of it. He was often the preferred partner for Democrats and Republicans across the ideological spectrum for many important issues, and his distinguished legislative record was because of who he was and not in spite of it. There was very good reason why a Democratic leader, Mike Mansfield of Montana, called him "the conscience of the Senate."

And while on the subject of the environment, another occasion vividly illustrates the senator's savvy political instincts, grace and sense of history.

The environment was my area of responsibility at the time I worked for Mac in 1973 and 1974, when the environment was awakening concern. "Saving the Bay" had become a watchword, and the senator was determined to make a real contribution.

The senator knew a key to making progress would be getting New York, Pennsylvania, Maryland, and Virginia together with a plan for the Bay. The Susquehanna River is the major freshwater inflow, and it starts in New York. Issues had arisen between Maryland and Virginia and the senator had asked Virginia's governor Linwood Holton to help move things along. The governor arranged for Mathias to come to Richmond to speak with legislative leaders and relevant members of his cabinet. I thought the next step would be for me to work on the trip's logistics and then drive with the senator to Richmond on the appointed day.

Senator Mathias had a better idea. One day he grabbed me from my desk, saying, "Follow me." As we headed down the hall I asked where we were going and for what purpose. "We are going to see Senator Harry Byrd about our trip to Richmond," and that was about all I was told. When we were ushered into Senator Byrd's office, he seemed equally in the dark as to the purpose of our visit. "Mac, this is a great pleasure; what in the world can I do for you?"

"Harry, my aide and I are thinking of crossing the Potomac to visit Richmond and would never do so without your permission and assurance of safe passage."

What then followed was a very amusing chat about previous instances of armies crossing the Potomac without permission, the nature of the visit and what Senator Byrd could do to ensure its success. I learned a lot that day about bipartisanship, courtesy and how the personal touch contributes to political success.

* * *

When it came to organizing his Senate office, descriptions like "benign neglect" or "the absent-minded professor" have some descriptive quality but only in their best sense. While Mac's touch may have been light on the tiller, there were principles governing the office on which he never wavered. He wanted bright, committed staff, and they had to have integrity. As one of his assistants, you always felt you were trusted, and it would have been a crushing blow to feel that you had let him down. He created an office based on culture and responsibility, not rules.

Let me start with things I learned on my first day in the office. At the first meeting of the legislative staff that I attended in September 1973, I was acquainted with what was described as the "proximity rule" for a legislative assistant working for Mac Mathias.

The rule was described by way of an illustration. "You'll be walking with the senator; he will have an idea; turn to you and issue specific instructions. The problem is that the subject will have nothing to do with your responsibilities or expertise. Even though the senator may issue very specific instructions, you are to do no such thing. Instead, tell the assistant whose area it is what the senator wants. If you instead follow the senator's instructions, you will have a very unhappy and possibly short career on his staff."

It wasn't long before there were ample opportunities for me to follow the proximity rule, and it wasn't the only aspect of office life that required getting used to.

All legislative assistants take up their duties with a vision of being engaged in the important issues of the day, winning great victories for worthy causes. Oh, were it so. Senator Mathias drove an old Buick that should have been reduced to scrap years before. One summer day I was sitting at my desk when he appeared and asked if I could follow him. We crossed the street to below the Senate steps of the Capitol where his car was parked with a very flat left front tire. What made the senator think of me for this assignment was unknowable and I couldn't figure a way to implement the proximity rule to involve someone else.

Soon we were hard at work, car jacked up, spare and tire iron ready, and down to our short sleeves. I'm pretty sure after that we agreed that the lug nuts holding the tire should be loosened in a counterclockwise direction. Certainly, my heroic efforts were at first in that direction. We then conferred and decided we should try the other way. Well, that sheared off a very rusted lug nut. I then tried the next nut in both directions and produced the same result.

Mathias didn't seem pleased with my work and took over. I couldn't have been happier that he was then able to duplicate my results. Sweating profusely, we retired to the Senate Office Building to call a towing service.

* * *

A Senate staffer's office life is not all research, hearings and constituent service. The senator had a farm near Frederick and on that farm were a pair of geese, until one day Mr. Fox came along and made a meal of Mr. Goose.

Mathias became concerned about how geese deal with such losses and whether it might ease the pain and loneliness if a new mate could be found. The staff sprang into action and I, because of subject matter expertise (environmental affairs), was in charge of finding a replacement goose. That mission was accomplished and a very large goose was procured.

We decided to make a presentation to the senator in his office with most staff present and a Senate photographer there to record this happy moment. I'd handled geese and this one in particular. The trick is to envelop their wings tightly with one arm and guard yourself from bites with the other.

Senator Mathias arrived for the presentation and brought along Senator Bob Taft, which was unplanned. The initial photo op with me presenting the goose to the senator went well. Then Mathias wanted a picture with him and Senator Taft holding the goose. I'm pretty sure I cautioned against this, and my last words were "Be careful."

As they posed for the picture, the goose got loose and in seconds had delivered painful blows to both senators, fled into and out of the fireplace and was now menacing the rest of the crowd, who were in flight mode themselves.

The goose eventually ended up at Mathias' farm and took up residence with the widow goose.

The farm where the new "Mr. Goose" took up residence was near and dear to Mac Mathias' heart. He also felt it was a valuable tie to the rural vote in Maryland. There was one little problem: the farm's actual location was in West Virginia.

Mathias often referred to his farm as "either near or outside of" Frederick, both because he loved it and because he thought Maryland voters would like him better as the senator from Frederick than from Chevy Chase or West Virginia.

The farm's actual location was as well guarded a secret as any he heard as a member of the Senate Intelligence Committee. At some point before the 1974 campaign a question arose as to what address should be used for his residency. Mathias wanted nothing to do with his home in Chevy Chase. In past campaigns he used a family address in Frederick, but his head hadn't touched the pillow there in many years. It was then that he revealed to some of us the secret location of Bullskin Farm.

I was given the job of seeing whether the old Frederick family address could still serve. I researched Maryland's election laws and consulted election experts. To my astonishment and the senator's glee, the laws of Maryland were sufficiently vague to allow the house in Frederick to be his residence.

* * *

Ann Mathias often, and on many occasions for good reason, viewed the Senate staff as detracting from her marriage. We never ceased our demands on the senator's time, and that made her a somewhat feared presence for many of us. Sometimes she had a point.

One day, Mrs. Mathias decided to have a ladies' lunch in the Senate dining room with the idea that the guests would meet in the senator's office before proceeding to lunch. At noon of the appointed day the ladies assembled. What happened next occurred behind closed doors and has remained the subject of differing accounts with varying attempts to apportion blame and punish the guilty.

It so happened that several months before this day, Senator Mathias had decided to restore his collection of leather-bound books on American and Maryland history. This involved an intern rubbing the books with some concoction of linseed oil and other oils, which were stored in an old sherry bottle.

By now you can guess the rest. The ladies, spying the sherry, suggested a pre-lunch aperitif, and once glasses were found and a toast proposed, the manure hit the fan. Senator Mathias' response was one of quiet humor when not in his spouse's presence and deep concern when she was around.

* * *

Unlike most senators, Mathias seemed to resist having a powerful administrative assistant to run his office. The most accepted theory was that a powerful AA could set the staff off in some direction without a proper sign-off from the senator. He kind of liked to be his own AA.

Since Senator Mathias' style of office administration bordered on benign neglect, having an ineffectual AA ensured that there would be plenty of debate and warning before consequential actions could be taken.

There came a time when a new AA was needed, and one arrived from another senator's office bringing with him his long-serving assistant—who also happened to be his partner. They intended to work as a team. Clearly, they hadn't read the memo on being "inconsequential." The office was soon bombarded with reorganizations, all centralizing power in these two individuals. Enough was enough, and the legislative staff met. We decided a direct confrontation was in order, and why not today with the senator conveniently out of town?

At the legislative staff meeting I was chosen as spokesman for the group. The reason given was that I was the least likely, many decided, for some reason, to be fired by the senator. With the passage of time I now realize that I was thought to be either the most expendable or not the sharpest knife in the drawer.

Anyway, the meeting with the AA was called for after lunch. He obligingly went over how he saw his recent changes and gave me the opportunity to say, "No, that isn't going to happen—etc." These comments caught his attention, and I was fired and told to vacate the office immediately.

My colleagues and I responded that I could only be fired by the senator. The rest of the afternoon can only be described as a ceasefire between two enemy camps.

Senator Mathias arrived back at his home on Leland Street late that night to find his new AA waiting on the lawn with the news that he had fired me. As reasons began tumbling out of his mouth, Mathias responded that it had been a long day and he was retiring.

We all came in the next day wondering what shoe would drop. Before lunch the staff received a note from the senator asking us to a picnic at his farm "near" Frederick on the coming Saturday. By Saturday it was all sorted. Most cars went fully loaded. I was going up in a car with my colleagues in the senior legislative group. The AA and his teammate were left to drive up together.

At lunch the senator talked about the important issues facing the country and the role he hoped to play with our help. Not a word or even passing reference to the office brouhaha. He then thanked us for coming. A month later we had a new AA and I never discussed the events of the week with the senator—not ever.

* * *

After several other Washington jobs I went back to Baltimore to practice law. In 1978 the senator asked me to be his campaign chair for the 1980 election, and I was honored to do so. Furlong Baldwin, Chair of the Mercantile Bank, headed the campaign's finance committee.

Baldy was hard-charging and sure of his opinions. He believed that we needed to raise lots of money and bury the opposition. We met with Senator Mathias monthly. Those meetings included pollsters, consultants and others, all with their hands out.

The meetings were like watching a relentless force meet an immovable object, with Baldy and the senator focused on a list of names where it had been decided that only the senator could make the calls.

Let me explain why the senator was the immovable object. Mathias loved being a senator. He disliked campaigning and he hated asking for money—absolutely hated it. Over the years he believed that he had developed a sensitive, very accurate internal system for arriving at just the right fundraising goal that would allow victory with a comfortable enough margin so as not to look vulnerable in the next election. He wasn't going to be involved in raising a dollar more. In fact, in his first bid for re-election to the Senate in 1974, Mathias vowed not to accept any contributions in excess of $100.

At each meeting Baldy would go down the list, and Mathias, with appropriate hemming and hawing, would fess up to having been distracted by important affairs of state so that no calls had been made. As a longtime observer of the Mathias method, it was a wonderful stroll down memory lane to see that nothing had changed since I left his staff.

* * *

After Senator Mathias retired from the Senate and was associated with a law firm, he would occasionally call me for dinner when he came to New York. One such occasion was in the late 1990s. A little before the appointed evening, he asked whether instead of going to a restaurant we could instead attend a dinner for the German Marshall Fund.

Our plan was for me to pick him up at the University Club, and in black tie we would go off to dinner. I was in the lobby at 7 and I began to worry by 7:20. Was he all right? Did I have the date wrong, or had he forgotten? A little later Mathias emerged from the elevator in his tuxedo but with his tie in hand.

Now in his 80s and experiencing somewhat less agility, tying a bowtie had proven very difficult for him. With good humor that I never could have equaled, Mac asked whether I could solve this "environmental" problem. After several failed attempts from the front my only hope was to try by standing behind him. I certainly did try, but the results were a disaster only rivaled by the flat tire incident of many years before.

Finally, the maitre d' came out of the dining room and took pity on us. As we went off to dinner, I reflected on how the trials that we had just endured had put the senator's strength of character and fundamental goodness on full display.

* * *

Being a U.S. senator is to live in a fishbowl, always on display. You are surrounded by constituents, the press, Senate colleagues and, most of all, your staff. The stories I have chosen, hopefully, provide some insight into Mac Mathias. His staff members and others could remember many other stories, and were those stories to be part of this essay, I am confident that they would reflect well on Mac Mathias. Even in times of stress, frustration or fierce partisanship, the senator set a high standard. He was wise, patient, caring and universally respected.

V. Successors

Team Maryland

SEN. BARBARA A. MIKULSKI (RET.)

I vividly recall the first meeting I had with Mac in 1976, after I was newly elected to the House of Representatives to take the seat vacated by Paul Sarbanes when he joined Mac in the Senate. Mac convened a meeting of the Maryland delegation with Senator Sarbanes and the other eight members in the House.

I was one of the "shiny brights" at the time. I went in dressed in my little bell bottoms, which were all the fashion then. Mac was the delegation's senior member, so he was our leader, even though he was a Republican leading a largely Democratic delegation.

Mac welcomed everybody, and he said these meetings were going to be different than in the past. One, he said, we're going to meet regularly, and two, there will be no smoking, no drinking, no card-playing. I was completely flabbergasted, coming as I did from the rough-and-tumble politics of East Baltimore, with characters like Mayor William Donald Schafer and the colorful councilman Mimi DiPietro. And this was after House delegations led by George Fallon and Samuel Friedel, who were interesting characters themselves. You know, I was a hidden smoker at the time—a few puffs here and there. But I certainly was willing to give that up if we were going to be pondering the world's problems.

Mac said it's always going to be "Team Maryland," kind of like NATO, with all the countries working together, and he added that "an attack on one will be considered an attack on all." So, if something came up in Washington in any of the agencies or in Congress, we would all work together for the best interests of the state. I thought to myself, "This is fantastic. He's everything I thought he would be."

Mac was very business-like. He established several committees. We would meet once a month. A member could bring up anything. He said we would invite the public on occasion, in a kind of a town hall format. We would also have meetings with statewide groups such as the National

Association of Community Colleges and veterans' groups. They had to meet statewide criteria, and they had to have an interest before the Congress and the federal government.

In running these meetings, he was never autocratic or heavy-handed; he was firm but very fair and didn't seem to care if you were a Republican or Democrat. He actively included the junior senator from Maryland, Paul Sarbanes. He was very congenial, and he was particularly inclusive of the women of the Maryland delegation—me, Marjorie Holt, Beverly Byron, and Gladys Spellman.

He felt a deep responsibility to serve the people of Maryland. I think that came from his family background in Frederick. His whole family identified themselves with Abraham Lincoln, especially on the issue of civil rights. He was a real champion. He was a Lincoln Republican like his fellow Republican colleagues, such as Senators Hugh Scott and John Heinz. He was devoted to his constituents, and whatever the project, he was determined that no issue or key decision would fall between the cracks.

Mac's deep concern for the people and problems of Maryland was remarkable—especially given how engaged he was in foreign policy, NATO, the Middle East, arms control, the Judiciary Committee and the Rules Committee. Mathias was a statesman, but I quickly learned that he could be quite the wheeler dealer as well. That's what we had to do. He effectively used his clout on the Appropriations Committee to be a champion for Maryland, its people and its institutions.

He was adept at working with everyone—and we had a very diverse delegation, from Republicans such as the Reagan conservatives Marjorie Holt and Bob Bauman to more progressive members such as Parren Mitchell and myself. And Mac had super contacts throughout the government, especially with the Pentagon and the State Department, that he would bring to bear on various matters.

* * *

Just as importantly, Mac was willing to take risks. He led the effort in Congress to restore the Chesapeake Bay and to establish the one and only EPA program for an estuary, ever! Along the way, he found a powerful ally across the aisle in Senator Sarbanes—a great expression of Team Maryland. It's a multistate program, which of course gave it added support in Congress, and it's considered a model for the nation. There were many delicate issues involved, including that we first had to work with—or try to work around—Anne Gorsuch, the Darth Vader of the EPA. But then, thankfully, she was replaced by the well-respected, less doctrinaire and more environmentally inclined William Ruckelshaus.

Mac loved the space program, a priority for both of us. As senators, we both held leadership positions on the Appropriations subcommittee that funded NASA, which of course is located in Goddard, Maryland. Mac's subcommittee appropriated the money for the Space Telescope Institute, and he led the delegation to try to get the institute located at the Johns Hopkins campus. We were competing with Princeton, the odds-on favorite at the time. Steve Muller, then the president of Johns Hopkins, was determined to get the institute. Mac, the delegation, Muller and Maryland officials out-organized and out-worked the New Jersey folks. And we won! This catapulted Johns Hopkins into a leadership position in astrophysics.

We all worked together. Not just on legislation, but on projects and contracts crucial to Baltimore and the state, especially protecting federal facilities and attracting new ones. Mac had considerable influence with the Pentagon, and Sarbanes was on the Banking Committee and later its chairman.

Team Maryland rallied together when Congress and the Carter administration were looking for a home for the new National Fire Academy. There was competition around the country, but Team Maryland won and got the academy located in western Maryland, at the former site of St. Joseph's College in Emmitsburg. It's really important to the economy out there.

Mac felt strongly about the needs of working people and their livelihoods. I remember when General Motors was forced to adapt to a new, changing economy. They had to retool, and they had to close plants and consolidate all around the country. They had announced plans to close the plant on Broening Highway in the Baltimore area, which meant we were going to lose jobs, 4,000 of them, a world of blue-collar jobs. Don Schaefer, the mayor of Baltimore, went ballistic. Mac and the delegation—we all worked together to cajole and persuade, to get the federal government to provide federal incentives, to stop GM from downsizing. We were working with the United Auto Workers, too. GM was so impressed with how well we in the Maryland delegation worked together, Democrats and Republicans as partners. We got GM to agree to stay a lot longer.

Fort Holabird, a Defense Intelligence Agency facility where spies were trained, was just across the street from GM. It was closed around the time of the first base closings in the 1970s. Mac, the mayor and the Maryland delegation wanted to save the jobs there and get the land, make it available for new enterprises. We wanted to get it cleaned up, to get all the environmental hazards removed, to make it a green field. Schaefer got the land deeded to the city. We were able to create an industrial park, and we helped get the federal funds we needed to make it work. It turned out to be a great economic tool to attract new industry. Today, Amazon is using that site, there's a biotech center there, and Baltimore is a thriving part of the Internet economy.

Another example—we were all set to get a new VA hospital in Baltimore, but we ran into a buzzsaw: President Reagan wanted to privatize veterans' hospitals throughout the country. Our Baltimore facility became a target, and Reagan impounded the money set aside to build it. After a president blocks money for something, getting it recovered is rare, but Team Maryland rallied and managed to get Congress to restore the money. That hospital has brought important benefits to the city—among other things, it's right next to the University of Maryland Medical Center and Hospital, and they have a great partnership. Steny Hoyer was very helpful as a member of the House Appropriations Committee, an example of how all the delegation members pulled together, even if their districts were not directly affected.

Mac not only led the effort to preserve the Bay, but he also made the Baltimore waterfront a priority. The Port of Baltimore employs a lot of people and is a crucial economic engine for the entire state. We made sure that Corps of Engineers money flowed to deepen the channel to 50 feet, enough to allow big ships to move coal and cargo to and from Baltimore and ensure that the city could remain a competitive port.

Mayor Schaefer was a pioneer, and he had a plan to redevelop Baltimore's Inner Harbor. Again, we all worked together to help him. Mac took the lead to get the Congress to designate the newly built Baltimore Aquarium, one of the best in the country, as the *national* aquarium. I did my part over in the House. Jimmy Carter was president; Pat Harris was secretary of HUD. Bob Embry, an imaginative former Baltimore official, was an assistant secretary of HUD and created the UDAG program, a federal-private partnership for redevelopment projects to revitalize cities. Mac and the delegation helped local leaders get UDAG grants. Mayor Schaefer and James Rouse, a visionary urban planner, developer, civic activist, and the father of Columbia and Harborplace, made full use of the money. The idea was to lure people back to downtown, and sure enough, the area eventually became a tourism mecca, well known as one of the best redevelopments in the country. The USS *Constellation* is docked there, and Mac helped get the money to restore it.

Mac was close to many of Baltimore's civic leaders and considered them confidants. Together they worked to help Baltimore on a range of projects, from redeveloping the Inner Harbor to helping grow higher education institutions. James Rouse was close to Mac. Walter Sondheim, a Baltimore businessman and well-known public servant, one of the leaders of the Baltimore waterfront development, was also part of his brain trust. Another friend was Furlong Baldwin, a banking powerhouse and

Baltimore Mayor William Donald Schaefer and Mathias on Baltimore's Harborplace (Mathias Family).

civic leader. Steve Muller, the president of Johns Hopkins, was also part of Mac's kitchen cabinet.

Mac and Sarbanes made a great team. They both made full use of their authorizing committees to set policy and create new programs to take care of Marylanders and the state. And Mac was very skillful in getting the needed money through the Appropriations Committee.

Mac and I had many of the same priorities—the space program, the Chesapeake Bay, bringing jobs to Maryland, helping Baltimore City, keeping and attracting federal facilities and a robust federal workforce, among others. So, when the time came, our transition in the Senate was seamless. These issues and projects require sustained efforts over many years. We needed—and we had—that kind of continuity.

* * *

Speaking of transitions, a day or two after I defeated the deeply conservative Linda Chavez in the 1986 election, Mac called and invited me to get together. He had an office in Baltimore, in the old Mercantile building, or perhaps it was an awful GSA building, and my House of Representatives office was in the same building.

He was the soul of civility; he gave me such a warm welcome. You have to remember I had run against him—and lost—in the 1974 election, a race I only got into because I thought Mac was going to lose in the Republican primary and that I would have a weaker opponent in the general election. But, of course, that didn't happen. The person I thought he would face in the GOP primary, Helen Bentley, chose to opt out.

When we met, he said, I want to say, three things: "One, thank God you won! I'm glad you are following me. You represent the values that I

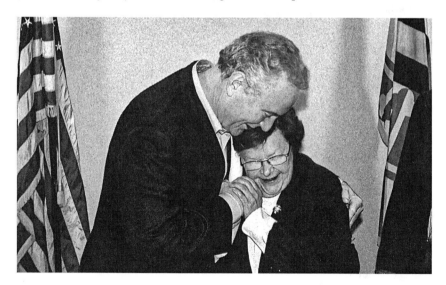

Senators Chris Van Hollen and Barbara Mikulski, successors to Senator Mathias (Senator Van Hollen files).

have fought for all my life. I loved your work in the House." He was so gracious.

Then he talked about constituent service and how important that was. "You must make sure that no person with a problem or complaint is overlooked," he said, adding that it was important to him to not just check the box, but that he had a duty to represent all Marylanders.

And third, he said, there were three issues that were most important to him, in addition to serving Maryland: the Chesapeake Bay, arms control and civil rights.

He knew my record pretty well and how much I was already working on civil rights and the empowerment of women—so we saw eye to eye on that.

It was a very orderly transfer of power, and I was forever grateful. He didn't treat it simply as one person taking over for another but as a careful changeover in which neither of us should want an important issue or project to fall through the cracks.

He also gave me great advice on managing constituent affairs—and just about all matters. He said I'd need a very strict manager to run my office. He emphasized how important it was to answer all the mail. I wound up hiring several people from his staff, and they all really helped me not to miss a beat, from getting the mail out to making sure we had enough paper clips. We used carbon copy paper in those days.

It was a real privilege to work in the Senate. I knew it then, but I appreciate it even more now. And from watching Mac from my seat in the House for all those years, I had a great lesson in how to be a senator. He was inspiring and a terrific example.

From Staffer to Successor

SEN. CHRIS VAN HOLLEN

In the summer of 1986, not long before Senator Charles Mathias retired, I attended a dinner held in his honor at the convention center in downtown Baltimore. At the time, I was working on his staff as a legislative assistant for defense and foreign policy. Ronald Reagan was president and Mikhail Gorbachev had recently become the leader of the USSR. Reflecting back on that evening reminds me why I consider Senator Mathias to be such an important role model to me.

The speakers that night talked at length about all the ways "Mac" had made an impact on the state of Maryland and our country during his more than three decades of public service, including nearly 20 years in the U.S. Senate—capturing his diverse interests and core values, including his strong lifelong commitment to civil rights and to environmental stewardship and the restoration of the Chesapeake Bay.

The event took place before a crowd of 1,300—including many colleagues from the Senate, friends from the U.S. House of Representatives, where he had served for eight years, and leaders from the civil rights, labor, business and diplomatic communities, as well as local and state Maryland leaders. One speaker, Juanita Jackson Mitchell, who came from a family of prominent civil rights activists and was the first African American woman to practice law in Maryland, recounted how she had worked with Mathias to develop a plan to integrate the opera house in Frederick when Mathias served as city attorney in western Maryland in the 1950s. Larry Simns, head of the Maryland Watermen's Association, told the assembled guests how Mathias was the only elected official who listened to him when he complained about the need to do something about the worsening pollution of the Bay in the 1970s.

One after the other, whatever the issue, the common theme that evening was that Mathias was a man of integrity who had the moral courage to judge issues on their merits and act on the strength of his convictions, regardless of the political consequences. Those virtues earned him the accolade "the conscience of the Senate" from Democratic Senate Majority leader Mike Mansfield.

I had long been interested in working on public policy issues, but my experience working for Senator Mathias provided me a front row seat to the arena where policy and politics intersect and planted the seed that led to my later decision to run for elected office myself.

When Mathias left the Senate in January 1987, I joined the Democratic staff of the Senate Foreign Relations Committee, but during my free time I had already started to get more involved in local Maryland issues. Two years later I left the Hill to work for William Donald Schaefer, then the governor of Maryland, as part of his D.C. office in the Hall of States, where my job was to focus on Maryland's federal priorities.

Then, in 1990, I ran successfully for the Maryland House of Delegates, and four years later I was elected to the Maryland State Senate, where I served two terms. In 2002—halfway through George W. Bush's first term, as the United States was moving to launch a war of choice in Iraq based on false premises—I ran for and was elected to the U.S. House of Representatives. Then, on November 8, 2016, I was elected to the U.S. Senate and won reelection in 2022. Other than my time in the Maryland Senate, it was much the same path Mathias had taken to the U.S. Senate nearly 50 years earlier.

* * *

All careers, including those in public policy and electoral politics, hinge on choices we make at certain junctures. In my journey, the first fateful decision I made was to pursue my interest in national security and defense policy.

As the son of a career Foreign Service officer, I spent many of my early years abroad. In every overseas post we served, the Cold War with the Soviet Union was the defining issue in our bilateral relationships. As time went on, I became increasingly aware of and concerned about the accelerating nuclear arms race and the potential for catastrophic miscalculation. The 1982 book *The Fate of the Earth* by Jonathan Schell provided the final impetus that led me to attend Harvard's John F. Kennedy School of Government to focus on international security and arms control issues.

In the spring of 1985, as I was completing my graduate degree, I learned of an opening in Senator Mathias' office for the position of legislative assistant for defense and arms control issues. My father had been born and raised in Baltimore and, while a Democrat, he had always admired Senator Mathias, who was more liberal than many of the Maryland Democratic elected officials who served during the 1960s and 1970s. And from

Senator Mathias and Chris Van Hollen, a member of the legislative staff in 1985 and 1986 (Senator Van Hollen files).

my perspective, Mathias would be a good fit because he was one of the most vocal proponents of using diplomacy and arms control agreements as part of an overall strategy to avoid a nuclear conflict that could end the world as we know it.

I was fortunate to land the job. Capitol Hill was an exciting place for a Senate staffer working on defense policy and nuclear arms control in the mid–1980s. The Berlin Wall was still very much in place and no one predicted that it would fall anytime soon. While the Reagan Administration was packed with many implacable foes of arms control agreements with the Soviet Union, Mathias was part of a small group of liberal Republican senators who were strong advocates for diplomacy and detente.

The Senate was closely divided in 1985—53 Republicans and 47 Democrats—often putting Mathias in a critical swing position. A review of his voting record shows that the year I joined his staff, Mathias was the Republican senator most likely to vote with the Democrats, which he did 51 percent of the time (on many occasions, however, his vote was counterbalanced by conservative Democrats voting with Republicans).

Mathias did his homework on every issue, including immersing himself in the details of foreign policy and national security matters. That gave him extra credibility on the key issues I was working on. I recall joining him in San Francisco for a meeting of the North Atlantic Assembly, a gathering of legislators and parliamentarians from NATO countries. While many members of the U.S. delegation were embarrassingly uninformed compared with their European peers, Mathias always saved the reputation of the American team with his deep knowledge of the players and the pressing issues of the day. He was a firm believer in the need for a strong Atlantic alliance to defend democratic values—and watching him in action, I came to more deeply appreciate the role of individual legislators in forging and maintaining those transatlantic relationships.

Even long after leaving the Senate, Mathias continued to work to nurture those ties. He was especially upset in 2003, when House Republicans implemented gratuitous measures to express their displeasure with those NATO partners who opposed President George W. Bush's decision to go to war in Iraq in 2003. The Republicans were in the majority in the House at the time, and they were especially angry at the French for their outspoken opposition to the U.S.-led invasion, so much so that they even banned the word "French" from the House dining room in the Capitol. They insisted on renaming French toast "Freedom toast" and French fries "Freedom fries."

Mathias' long experience with the French had made him something of a Francophile, so when he heard of this, he was irritated. He called me and said, "Chris, I want you to get to work on changing this, and you should join the French Caucus." I agreed with him. France and all our NATO partners had rallied behind us to invoke Article 5 of the NATO Charter after al Qaeda's 9/11 attack and supported our mission in Afghanistan, but I shared their opposition to the war in Iraq. And so, at Mathias's urging, I joined the French Caucus and when the Democrats regained control of the House in 2007, we returned the "French" to their rightful places on the House menu.

I was also following the Mathias example when, after I was sworn into the Senate in 2017, I decided to band together with eight Senate colleagues to re-launch the bipartisan NATO Observer Group. The group's purpose was to work with fellow elected officials from NATO countries to strengthen ties. The previous iteration of the group had dissolved years before, but President Trump's open hostility toward NATO motivated us to re-establish it in order to demonstrate the Senate's bipartisan commitment to the importance of our transatlantic partnership. Mathias, who passed away in 2010, would have been smiling. In a similar fashion, I thought of Mathias again when I attended the Munich Conference for the third time in February 2022—just as Vladimir Putin began mobilizing his forces to prepare for Russia's attack against Ukraine. Mathias' constant exhortations about the need to cultivate and preserve the NATO Alliance could not have been more prescient than at that moment.

Mathias' credibility and expertise on national security issues also made him a natural partner for other senators interested in those issues. For example, he teamed up with Ted Kennedy to introduce legislation, Senate Joint Resolution 179, to request that the president resume negotiations with the Soviet Union on a verifiable comprehensive test ban treaty. The Reagan administration opposed the measure, and despite the efforts of myself and Kennedy's staff, Republicans and some Democrats maneuvered procedurally to prevent its passage. On other matters, the bipartisan coalitions were more successful. Fred Hill, Mathias' director of foreign affairs, and I worked long hours with several Democratic senators' legislative assistants to shape an appealing compromise on the Anti-Apartheid Act, the sanctions against the White minority regime in South Africa. Due to that bipartisan effort, the legislation passed a Republican-controlled Senate overwhelmingly over sitting Republican President Reagan's veto— something that is impossible to imagine ever happening today.

During my time as a U.S. senator, I have followed Mathias' lead in seeking to work across the aisle on many foreign policy and national security matters. Even in these polarized times, I have been able to forge fruitful bipartisan partnerships on some of those key issues. And I think of Mac Mathias on those occasions.

Working for Mathias deepened my knowledge of national security and foreign policy issues but, just as importantly, my two years as a legislative assistant to a respected senator gave me a vital education in how Congress actually works. On one of my first days on the job, I was preparing to make a recommendation to Mathias on how to vote on a particular issue. I had diligently prepared myself. When the voting bells rang, I joined him outside his Russell Building office and walked with him as he started to make his way toward the senate Chamber. I began going through the long list of the pros and cons on the issue as they might be laid out in a graduate school thesis, proud of my thorough grasp of the matter. The senator, though, paused, looked at me and, with a sly smile, asked, "How is Jesse Helms going to vote on this?" I said, "Senator, he's going to vote nay." The senator responded, "Then I'm a yea!"

Senator Helms, a controversial and outspoken Republican from North Carolina, was one of the most conservative members in the Senate, and he and Mathias were reliably on opposite sides of most issues. The moment Mathias asked me how Helms would vote, I had no doubt that he had already educated himself on the matter. His question to me was a gentle instruction to quickly get to the heart of the matter. As time went on I came to recognize that, since senators had to juggle hundreds of issues at once, being able to cut to the core of the issue was a job requirement for any staff member—and any member of Congress.

When I was elected to the House of Representatives, I used this technique to urge my staff to quickly get to the point, but instead of asking how Helms would vote, I substituted Representative Tom DeLay, the conservative Republican whip and lightning rod from Texas.

Mathias set an example not only through his work but also through how he lived his life. He was a senator who never let his title or position go to his head. He was unpretentious in a body that has an overabundance of preening, outsized egos. One of my favorite symbols of that was the vehicle he chose to drive, a broken down, rattletrap 1966 Buick station wagon that the staff dubbed the "Blue Bomber."

I remember a road trip I took with him to what was then called the Wilson School of Public and International Affairs at Princeton University, where he was to give a talk. As he drove through parts of Maryland, he recounted the history of our state, including the role the French had played in helping save the American Revolution (another reason he was so offended by the anti–French actions of the House Republicans during the Iraq war). But in the middle of this history lesson we got stuck in a big northbound traffic jam on I-95 with time running short before his scheduled remarks. And so, very calmly and without a hint of frustration, he turned the Blue Bomber across the grassy gully of the median, got onto the southbound lanes, and then took the next exit, proceeding along back roads until we reached Princeton on time.

Mathias' unassuming manner but effective legislating is one of the things that drew me to his office in the first place. Politically, it might seem at first blush as if I was a mismatch for the office: I was a staunch Democrat, and he was a lifelong Republican. But being from a different party didn't matter that much, at least not in those days working for him. We had similar values on core issues, saw eye to eye in the areas I was working on, and he was an individual of principle. But just as important, the Republican Party was very different then—there were hard-core conservatives like Helms, of course, but some Republicans were more liberal, like Mathias. At the same time, when I started working for him in 1985, many Senate Democrats were much more conservative than he was. By the time I joined his staff, Mathias had already organized a group known as the "Gang of Six," which, in addition to him, included Robert Stafford of Vermont, Lowell Weicker of Connecticut, John Chafee of Rhode Island, Mark Hatfield of Oregon and Mark Andrews of North Dakota. They were all liberal, independent-minded Republican senators who worked closely with the Democrats on many key matters, including the issues I worked on, national security and arms control. Today, Republicans like the Gang of Six are an extinct species in the Senate.

What was so special about Mathias was that he was truly of "the party of Lincoln," as the GOP likes to call itself in honor of the first president elected as a Republican. That stands out to me because of his leadership and the key role he played on civil rights, voting rights, and the legislation to impose tough anti-apartheid sanctions on South Africa.

If you look at the evolution of America and politics in this country, you can trace a lot back to the civil rights movement. Just weeks before the November 1960 election, Dr. Martin Luther King, Jr., found himself locked in a Georgia prison cell. John F. Kennedy was a candidate for president and there was a heated debate within his campaign about whether Kennedy—fearful of losing the then-segregationist Southern Democrats—should call Dr. King's wife, Coretta Scott King, to express his sympathy and solidarity. It's hard today to imagine that being a controversial decision, but when Kennedy did make the call, he was identifying himself openly with the civil rights movement and with the aspirations of Black Americans. When LBJ became president and signed the landmark 1964 Civil Rights Act, he accurately predicted that the Democrats would lose the South to Republicans for generations. This was a watershed moment in American politics.

Mathias played an important role in crafting the 1964 Act, in league with John Lindsay of New York and William McCulloch of Ohio. They took it upon themselves to introduce a civil rights bill. Their initiative spurred the Kennedy administration to finally get a bill drafted. Mathias played a major role in its passage one year later. He was also an important actor in the approval of the Voting Rights Act of 1965.

I didn't join Mathias' staff until his final two years in the Senate, but I was aware of his record of service. I knew that when he ran for reelection, he not only won the endorsement of civil rights groups, but he was also endorsed by labor organizations. This shows how much politics have changed in Maryland—today you'd be hard pressed to find Republicans having broad support from the civil rights community or widespread support from labor unions.

Mathias was firmly rooted in the party of Abraham Lincoln, but Republicans today have chosen a different path—one that led them to become the party of Donald Trump. Whenever Mathias talked about the modern Republican party after he retired, he would always harken back to Lincoln, noting wistfully that Republicans used to be the party of civil rights. Mathias would still be a good fit for Maryland today, but he would not be able to run as a Republican because his party left him long ago.

What we all admired about Mathias was the fact that he stuck to his principles, despite the political forces working against him. And he got punished politically for sticking to those principles. GOP leaders denied him the chairmanship of the Senate Judiciary Committee he was in line for because they didn't want a Republican like him using the post to guide changes on social justice issues.

Mathias also focused intently on regional and local matters of special importance to Maryland. At the top of that list was protecting our national treasure, the Chesapeake Bay. He is considered the "father of the Chesapeake Bay program" because when the Bay was in real danger of dying, he started the EPA-led, federal-state partnership to clean it up, which became a model for the nation and has persisted to this day. I've been working on the Bay cleanup since I was first elected to the Maryland state legislature and I can see the progress, but it's clearly a long-term project. Mathias had the foresight to recognize that because the Bay watershed encompasses six states and the District of Columbia, the federal government has an essential role to play in coordinating clean-up efforts and providing federal resources. His staff person on the Bay, Monica Healy, worked with him to secure federal resources, and since I have been in the Congress, I have worked to keep the momentum going, secure federal resources, and carry the torch that Mathias lit.

When Mathias announced his retirement in 1986, a scrappy fighter from Fells Point, Barbara Mikulski, then a five-term member of the House, ran for and won the Senate seat he had held. Senator Barb, as she is fondly known, represented Maryland in the Senate for the next 30 years, earning a well-deserved reputation as someone who stood up for working folks and used her perch on the powerful Senate Appropriations Committee to deliver results for the people of Maryland.

When Senator Mikulski decided not to run for re-election in 2016, I ran for and won the Senate seat earlier held by the man I had worked for. The Senate I was sworn into was a very different place than the one Mathias left in January 1987. The Republican purge of liberal Republicans like Mac was long complete, and the night I was first elected to the Senate was also the night Donald Trump was elected to the presidency, casting a dark pall over our celebration.

Many books have been written about what has happened in American politics over those 30 years, and many more will surely come. This is not the time or place for me to analyze what transpired. I do hope, however, that aspiring elected officials throughout Maryland and the nation will learn about the story and service of Mac Mathias. I still have one of his old campaign posters with the proud tagline "Maryland's voice of conscience"—and that accurately captures what he was all about. He listened carefully to his constituents and genuinely considered everyone's opinions, but at the end of the day, he had a strong North Star guiding him. He was a man of principle and political courage and an independent thinker. He was a hard worker, with a sense of humility, who did not seek out the glitz and limelight but worked every day to get the job done for his state and for our country. I know that in at least in one measure, I have succeeded in emulating him: my children have lamented the fact that I have the same theory about cars as he did about the Blue Bomber—run them until they stop.

Above all, the Mathias model was that connection to family is the key to staying grounded. He loved his family and benefited greatly from their support. His wife Ann, and their two sons, Charles and Robert, made sure the title "senator" never went to his head, and he valued their input and insights in everything he did. I was honored to be asked by his family to be a pallbearer at his memorial service. In that small way I was able to say a final goodbye to a good and honorable man, a mentor, and, later, a friend, a man who lived by his principles regardless of the consequences and continues to inspire me today.

Appendix 1

Eulogy at February 2, 2010, Memorial
Service at the National Cathedral
by Vice President Joseph Biden

Ann, Charlie, Rob, Sarah, and your magnificent granddaughters, Clare and Catie, remember what I told you, girls—no boys till you're 30. You had a wonderful grandfather.

We are here today to celebrate—but I must say we also mourn with you. It is a tough time when you lose a father, husband, so devoted, grandpa.

The U.S. Senate, many of whom are here, former members, and present members, the State of Maryland, the entire country mourns with you. We understand we have lost a great man, a fierce leader, a believer in right, good and truth.

In a sense, I lost a fellow who was a mentor of mine when I first came to the Senate as a 29-year-old kid. You were saying, Rob, that your dad, or maybe it was Charlie, he taught you patience, kindness and humility.

I got most of them, except for the patience part. He really had to work awfully hard on me on that one.

I served with Mac for 14 years. Many have served longer that are sitting here.

They were my first years in the Senate. I learned long after he left our chamber that the whole time I served with him he was truly looking out for me. He had taken me under his wing.

I guess I kind of knew that from the first time I met your mom and dad. Ann, you might remember this. It was in January 1973. I had just made it to the Senate a little later than most of my colleagues, because I came a little late. We were riding a bus—I was riding a bus with Ann and Mac from Austin, Texas, where we had just attended a memorial service for President Johnson. The bus was heading to his ranch in Stonewall,

Vice President Biden (at left in the first row) before delivering the eulogy at the memorial service for Senator Mathias at the National Cathedral, February 2, 2010. To his left are Ambassador Nigel Steinwald, United Kingdom; Senator Paul S. Sarbanes; Walter Pincus; and Ann Pincus. In the second row from left are Senator Chris Dodd (D–CT); Senator Benjamin Cardin (D–MD); and Representative Steny Hoyer (D–MD). In the third row from left are Senator John Warner (R–VA) and Senator Barbara Mikulski (D–MD) (Baltimore Sun Media. All Rights Reserved).

Texas, for the burial. It was only about an hour's ride. But in that hour I learned a lifetime's worth. I learned about the profound depths of compassion and the towering heights of dignity of your mother and father. Ann, you were so kind to me on that ride.

In that short ride on that bus, I learned what it meant to serve my country with a keen mixture of ferocity and grace. I learned what it meant to lead. I remember getting off the bus and feeling better about being in the Senate.

As Ann will remember, I didn't want to come to the Senate. I had just lost my wife and daughter in an automobile accident and my two boys were still hospitalized. The way you put your arms around me, literally and figuratively, Ann, and the way Mac embraced me, it was when it became clear to me that, Charlie and Rob, both our dads had something in common about the word perseverance. I was politely told, with a great deal of warmth and comfort, that it was about persevering.

I remember getting off the bus, as we boarded the plane, thinking, I hope I can meet the lofty standards of the couple who I had ridden two hours with, to and from Stonewall.

From Mac, more than anything else, I learned about courage, both moral and political courage. As Vicky knows, an oft quoted Robert Kennedy line—and I heard Ted Kennedy use it—"Moral courage is a more rare commodity than bravery in battle or great intelligence." Mac served his country in a communications ship in the Pacific in World War II. As Charlie and Rob have pointed out, and all we who worked with him knew, he had a keen intellect—gained from the time he spent at Haverford, Yale and Columbia—which was second to none. I used to kid him and say, the only reason he is not a Democrat is because he went to Yale.

It is most of all about Mac's moral courage, the rarest of commodities, that made him stand out from many of the great men and women with whom I have served. As I was telling Ann in the vestibule, when I left the Senate, after I had been elected seven times, the Senate historian pointed out to me, thinking I'd be flattered, that only 17 men in the history of the U.S. Senate have served longer than I have. All I could hear was my father's phrase that that was the definition of a misspent adulthood. The reason I mention that is not because I lasted for a long time, but because I met a lot of great women and men with whom I served. When I speak of Mac and his moral courage, it is not as a casual observer. I had been there since 1972.

Mac had that most rare of commodities, moral courage. It made him stand out from many of the great women and men with whom I have served. He had a value set that he refused to walk away from. In today's political environment, people would run away from [it] in order to save their political skins. Everybody forgets that as difficult as these days are, as Rob pointed out, the 1960s were equally as difficult. In fact, they may have been more difficult and required greater clarity and moral courage.

We were at one of those great inflection points in American history. Fortunately, we had men like Mac and Teddy Kennedy, and others I won't begin to name because I might leave someone out. Political expediency, in my observation, never meant anything to Mac. Moral compromise meant even less. I will not recount, as I have intended to do, because of the wonderful remembrances thus far.

But think about it. Mac voting against and coming out against the Vietnam War when incredible pressure was being placed on him as a loyal

Republican. Mac, marching with Gloria Steinem and Bella Abzug. In the midst of a highly charged atmosphere, when most people were hoping to not have to talk to either one of them with the cameras on because they were such lightning rods. Wonderful people, but such political lightning rods for significant parts of our constituency. Mac just went out and marched with them.

Campaigning for campaign finance reform—oh, God, had he won. What a different country this would be if he had prevailed on campaign finance reform. Watergate—not a very popular position as a leading Republican. I served with Mac on the Judiciary Committee and Foreign Relations Committee for the entire 14 years that we served together. Watching him step up on issue after issue, I wondered how in God's name can he survive, particularly with political representation, with the political party he belonged to at the time. As the bishops pointed out to me, it was noted that he voted with Republicans 31 percent of the time. I used to kid your dad and said he was really a Democrat but for his pedigree. All this French stuff threw him off. My middle name was Robinette. But I overcame that to be a Democrat.

All kidding aside, you have read a lot since his death about how he reached across the aisle. I never thought of Mac reaching across the aisle, I thought of him as never even recognizing there was an aisle. I never thought of him as having to go out of his way to reach across. It was who he was. There was no artificial divide. There was only principle. He approached every issue with his principles firm, but, unlike many today and even then, with his mind open. He had an open mind and would approach every issue that way. To Mac, right and wrong were not defined by whether or not you had a D or an R placed after your name. You were defined by what was in your heart. Mac never let any other force guide him but that one.

I rely here on the words of Ralph Waldo Emerson, who said, "Whatever course you decide upon, there is always someone to tell you you're wrong, there are always difficulties arising tempting you to believe your critics are right. To map out a course of action and follow it to the end requires courage." It seemed to me your father never had a doubt about what course he would set. It seemed to me that it was just almost instinctive with him, although he could articulate it in ways that are beyond my capabilities. He had his critics and heard doubts from others. But he harbored no doubt that I could observe about what he believed, no reservations about his core principles: freer people, a fairer system, equality for everyone, not just here in the United States, but around the world.

I remember one time, Charlie, I was just sort of disappointed in your dad, but then I realized his wisdom was carrying him. We had George

Shultz—you'll remember this encounter, Paul—testifying before our committee, a great man. We were having a hearing on apartheid. Secretary Shultz was making the administration's argument that we should not impose sanctions. I got very upset with a comment he made. I said I am ashamed of this administration. Before Paul could get to me, who is usually my governor, a note from Mac got slipped across the chairman to me saying, "Calm down, big fella." Like I said, you learned patience better than I did, boys.

I remember going to his office afterward. I was angry and fuming about this injustice. I thought Mac, who along with Teddy and others were my heroes in terms of civil rights—how could he have not just eaten this guy alive for what he was saying?

I walked into his office and there was a beautiful, lovely dog—actually, I kind of liked that beast. If my memory serves me correctly, he had a little table in front of his desk with a tea set on it. He got up from behind his desk in his rumpled suit. I was still fuming. He walked around and he poured a cup of tea and said, "Sit down, Joe. This will help you."

Then he began to say to me, Colby, in effect, they cannot get you for what you do not say. Joe, you are saying too much. I understand your heart.

The Mathias family entering the memorial service at the National Cathedral, February 2, 2010. Ann Bradford Mathias and Charles Mathias are in the front, and Sarah and Rob Mathias are in the back. Sarah and Rob's daughters, Catie and Clare, are in the middle (Baltimore Sun Media. All Rights Reserved).

And then he went through it with me. He not only made me feel better when I walked out, but he ended up leading the fight that succeeded to get the very objective accomplished that I cared deeply about.

Ann, one of the measures on how you're in sync with a man or a woman is whether or not the people that you admire the most are similar if they're mutual acquaintances. For Mac, and in my case, those people were identical. *The Times* last week listed the senators he most admired: J. William Fulbright, Mike Mansfield, Philip Hart, John Sherman Cooper, Jake Javits, George Aiken and Clifford Case. That is my list, too, except I would add Mac Mathias.

These men formed the intellectual and moral compass of the United States in my early years of the Senate. They came from different parties and different backgrounds, but shared one thing in common. They believed in basic human decency, gender and racial equality. They belonged to a political party, but they were patriots first. Instead, they viewed themselves, as I observed them—and I knew all of them except for Senator Cooper—they started from the premise that they represent the American people.

Mac was part of the moral compass and his true North pointed toward what was best for the people of Maryland and our country and the world.

People today think that to march out of lockstep with your political party and to speak out independently is some sort of a new form of courage. Folks, it has been around a long time, it has just been in pretty rare supply these days. It has always been in rare supply. It was in rare supply then.

Mac was speaking out independently a generation ago. If he did not invent what it meant to be independent of mind in the United States, he helped define and master it.

On top of all that, Mac was always a gentleman, graceful without pretense. He would have a way of calming things, without in any way backing down from how deeply he felt about an issue or principle. He was calm all the time, at least in my observation. He was the calm in the center of the storm and there were many storms in those first 14 years when I was around. He was the voice of reason, at times when reason itself was a very rare commodity.

I like to think of him, having suffered greatly from a horrible disease, as being in a much better place now. Hopefully, when it is our time to join him there, he will greet us with a warm smile, calmly standing up in his rumpled suit, pour us a glass of tea and say, "Settle down and welcome."

You are already missed. I think you're looking down on us, old buddy—"Stay calm, Joe"—and I implore you to send a little of your steadfast belief in unity and common cause and ideals that transcend politics and breathe it into the souls of our friends on the Hill, and keep reminding me, as well.

May your spirit guide us all, Mac. Those of us who knew and loved you will be forever pulled along by your undying decency that laid at the heart of everything you did.

Ann, when I think of Mac, I think that the British poet and historian Thomas Macaulay must have had him in mind when he wrote, "The measure of a man's real character is what he would do if he knew he would never be found out."

Mac's one of the men that I am absolutely confident would have acted no differently under any of the trying circumstances he participated in, even if he knew he would never be found out.

Thank God we found out and had an opportunity to know how decent a man he was. He could not have done it without you, Ann. You are a lady, and I am honored to know you. Thank you for asking me to be here.

Appendix 2

In His Own Words:
Excerpts from Speeches and Testimony

With his lifelong admiration for Abraham Lincoln, Senator Mathias was a student of American history, well read, keenly aware of its conquests, compromises and conflicts. He was fond of reading George Washington's farewell address on the floor of the U.S. Senate on the first president's birthday. He read it on the floor year after year, often to a nearly empty chamber.

Following are notable remarks, quotations, historical references and poignant comments on American history, foreign affairs, political life and society by the senator during his 28 years in elected office.

American History

"So, I propose that we make this Sesquicentennial Anniversary of the birth of Abraham Lincoln a day of dedication to the kind of life Lincoln lived—a life guided by principle and personal conviction. If we do, there may be a new birth of freedom. We may make it possible for our successors to look back to our own generation and say of us on future anniversaries of this day: In that time, the American dream was realized and American greatness was achieved by men of principle—men in the mold of Lincoln!"
—*The Lesson of Lincoln, House of Delegates,*
Annapolis, February 13, 1959

"It was not his genius but his principles that raised Lincoln so far above his own day and generation. And this may be the lesson of Lincoln— that each of us must live by and for our principles, or her convictions."
—*Lincoln Day Speech, House of Delegates,*
Annapolis, 1960

"During my years in the Congress, three historic events tested the foundations of the Republic: the Civil Rights movement, the Vietnam War and Watergate. Cumulatively and individually they might have destroyed our society, but they did not. We came through that time of challenge not destroyed, but actually strengthened as a nation and as a people. And we came through strong, not because of any single person or any group of people, but because of the rational principles of government laid down for us two hundred years ago by those exceptional men who wrote the Constitution."

—Speech at tribute to his career, Baltimore, July 14, 1986

The Constitution and the Rule of Law

"If we ever depend upon one man to sustain the law for us, then the rule of law will end, and a tyranny, however benevolent, will commence."

"The law in America has traditionally served us as both a shield and a sword—a shield to protect our citizens and our civilization, and as a sword to strike down injustices, inequities, and arbitrary uses of power and force."

—U.S. House of Representatives, August 15, 1967

"The only way to restore confidence and trust throughout our society is for everyone who shares the privilege of leadership to obey the law, and to meet the small questions and the great issues with equal courage."

—U.S. Senate, March 29, 1973

Civil Rights and Voting Rights

"The protection and extension of basic human rights in America and around the world must never disappear from the public agenda. More and more we will discover that the measure of our civilization will be taken from how we protect and provide for minorities and the disadvantaged."

—Advice to successors upon announcing retirement,
September 25, 1986

"The single garment of destiny, woven for us by Martin Luther King Jr., is called reconciliation. [His] achievement, which was a goal that eluded such great presidents as Abraham Lincoln and Theodore and Franklin Roosevelt, was to bring about a unity of the American people, Black and White. When you see evidence of that unity, evidence of national reconciliation, you see his monument."

—Dedication of Martin Luther King, Jr., Memorial Bust,
U.S. Capitol, January 16, 1986

American Democracy and Its Challenges

"There are two unmistakable trends working against the democratic balance. One is the decline of voter participation. The other is the rise of special interest influence."

—*Haverford College, January 27, 1983*

Congress

"There's always the story that when a member of the House is elected to the Senate, it raises the intellectual level on both sides, in both houses."

—*Interview with the Miller Center Foundation*
and Edward M. Kennedy Institute

[Asked about legislative maneuvers to defeat efforts by Senator Jesse Helms (R–NC) to block legislation to establish a national holiday for Martin Luther King, Jr.]: "[We] just froze [him] out. [We] ignored him. The most effective thing in politics is to be ignored."

—*Interview with the Miller Center Foundation*
and Edward M. Kennedy Institute

Political Labels

[Addressing the frequent description of him as an "independent"]: "My own philosophy is that, first and foremost, I am in the Senate to represent the people of Maryland, all the people. Second, I believe that the people of the state have elected me not with a view to holding a referendum every time a critical question comes up ... but to use my head and be guided by my conscience."

—*B'nai B'rith, Montgomery County, Maryland, October 21, 1974*

Foreign Affairs

"An American foreign policy does not need to be manipulative or brutal to succeed. What is required in our foreign policy leaders is a deep understanding of the history, behavior, policies and resources of other nations and peoples, and even more important a full understanding of the purposes of the Constitution, the course of American history and the beliefs of the American people."

—*City Club, San Diego, January 9, 1973*

"As a people we have stumbled out of the Vietnam nightmare scarred and embittered, but thanks to constant exercise, our civil liberties were still strong."

—*University of Maryland, February 17, 1977*

"The one, perhaps the only, common vital interest of the United States and the Soviet Union is that we do share both the planet and the capacity to destroy all the life on it. We need, therefore, to develop some rules to keep our other interests in check, to insure that our rivalry does not become a fatal one. It is imperative that the United States and the Soviet Union acquire the ability to conduct a civil conversation with each other."

—*World Affairs Council, Orange County, California,*
December 13, 1983

"Foreign relations are not a card game. They are a deadly serious business. The world is not peopled with mythical dragons and eagles and polar bears, but with human beings who yearn for peace and security and the necessities of life. We must seek to compose our differences with both China and the Soviet Union...."

—*Model United Nations, February 22, 1979*

"The Reagan administration's Middle East policy, or what is left of one after Lebanon, failed peace talks, shelved arms sales, etc. ... brings to mind one of Mark Twain's maxims about learning through experience. A cat that sits down on a hot stove lid, said Twain, 'will never sit down on a hot stove lid again, and that is well; but also she will never sit down on a cold one.'"

"During a three-week trip to the Middle East in February 1986, I found telltale signs that in the last few years the United States has, like Twain's cat, learned the wrong—or too many—lessons from its recent experiences ... and now seems reluctant to come near the source of the pain with anything like the full-fledged commitment that previous administrations thought necessary to ward off potential conflicts and promote peaceful solutions in one of the world's most critical regions."

—*"Dateline Middle East,"*
Foreign Policy *magazine, Summer 1986*

"The 'secret weapon' of ethnic interest groups is neither money nor technique, which are available to other interest groups, but the ability to galvanize for specific political objectives the strong emotional bonds of large numbers of Americans to their cultural or ancestral homes."

—*"Ethnic Groups and Foreign Policy,"*
Foreign Affairs, *Summer 1981*

"Granting these benefits, ethnic politics, carried out as they often have been to excess, have proven harmful to the national interest. Bearing out George Washington's warning, they have generated both unnecessary animosities and illusions of common interest where little or none exists."

—*"Ethnic Groups and Foreign Policy,"*
Foreign Affairs, *Summer 1981*

Senator Mathias and members of his personal legislative staff and staffers on his Senate committees, which included Foreign Relations, Judiciary and Rules, 1986. The senator is shown at position #1. Contributors to this book pictured include Monica Healy (#2), Ann Terry Pincus (#3), Randolph Marshall Collins (#4), Chris Van Hollen (#5) Steven J. Metalitz (#6), and Casimir Yost (#7) (Mathias Family).

Cities

"Our aim must be to create urban environments which will take their character from the human needs of the people who live in them. We must make cities where people can live and raise their children in dignity.... We are not doing this now."

—*Cleveland City Club, February 6, 1976*

Diversity and Immigration

"From the earliest migrations ... America has been repeatedly strengthened and enriched by the infusion of new talents and energies. The tired and poor, the homeless and tempest-tossed ... became, within a generation or two, the scientists and entrepreneurs, the farmers and skilled laborers, the artists and writers who have made America the model and envy in so many respects of the whole world."

—*"Ethnic Groups and Foreign Policy,"* Foreign Affairs, *Summer 1981*

Character

"You are going to write many letters on my behalf. All I ask is that when you look at what you have written just be sure that you wouldn't mind if it appeared on the front page of *The Washington Post.*"

—To legislative assistant Stuart Janney

"I will really miss the ability to pick up the telephone and do something for someone's life."

—Response to a reporter's question at the 1986 retirement tribute on what he will "miss most" about the Senate

Appendix 3

In Their Own Words: Remarks from Others

On July 14, 1986, approximately 1,300 of Senator Mathias' friends, colleagues and constituents gathered at the Baltimore Convention Center to honor the senator not long after his decision to retire. This brief collection of tributes captures the deep respect and admiration of so many throughout Maryland, the United States and the world's diplomatic community for his exemplary service to the country—from his career in the U.S. Navy during World War II to his political representation of Maryland and American interests as a member of the House of Representatives and the Senate for 26 years.

James Rouse, the noted builder and lifelong community leader, was the master of ceremonies. He kicked off the proceedings, saying to the invited speakers—ranging from senators to ambassadors, mayors and governors to civil rights leaders, farmers, watermen and labor leaders, "We will see Mac Mathias as a great, kind, reasonable man, of deep human values with an abiding sense of history, with sparkling common sense and independent thought and action."

* * *

"Mac's greatest legacy may be that he has stood for principle above politics. Some say that for his independence of thought he is a man without a party. But I think history will show he is a man of both parties. Indeed, Charles Mathias may be the rare senator who is a man above the party."

—*Harry Hughes, Governor of Maryland*

"No matter who you are—a member of Congress, dignitary, rich or poor, young or old—[Mac Mathias] takes time to listen, to be concerned, to be interested and to help to bring about a better quality of life for all Americans." [Noting the senator's many accomplishments, including programs to fight poverty, promote economic development of Baltimore and legislation to restore the Chesapeake Bay]: "One of the things that you like about a man like that, he was always quick to share and to give credit rather than take it for himself, and that's one of the reasons for his greatness."

—*William Donald Schaefer, Mayor of Baltimore*

[Recalling Mathias' early decision as city attorney for his home city of Frederick to desegregate the city's opera house]: "Mac, we have come a long way in Maryland. Clarence and I have 12 grandchildren, we even have a little boy who thinks he'd like to be president. They have such hope in their eyes. So, Mac, we thank you—they will help to make [the America we hope and dream of] because you paved the way."

—*Juanita Jackson Mitchell, civil rights leader*

"For more than 30 years, Mac has been steadfast in his commitment to the vision of our Founding Fathers. His eloquent advocacy of humane values, his deep belief in the words inscribed above the Supreme Court, 'equal justice under law,' have elevated our national life and made a singular contribution to a just and decent society."

—*Senator Paul S. Sarbanes (D–MD)*

"Wise and discriminating, you have debated the issues of the day with measured purpose and a twinkle in your eye. I have tended to believe this is because the measured purpose stems from a great love, respect and a keen appreciation for history and for the land."

—*Senator Nancy Kassebaum (R–KS)*

"Mac Mathias, perhaps more than any member of Congress I have known, exemplifies that independence and separateness [of the role of Congress]. His understanding of the speciality of his constitutional role, his ability to joust with presidents, to agree with his colleagues and to disagree on great issues."

—*Senator Howard Baker (R–TN)*

[Recalling a boat trip organized by Senator Mathias to inspect the declining condition of the Chesapeake Bay in the 1970s and crediting Mathias with standing up to corporate interests to rally support for its recovery]: "He started that ball rolling, and it was like a snowball. He never stopped. He kept right on driving that snowball to make it bigger. He got the public involved and all the politicians involved, and now we are on the way to saving the Bay."

—*Larry Simns, President of the Maryland Watermen's Association*

[Prefacing his comments by noting that he really should be in Washington celebrating France's national day, Bastille Day, and raising a toast to the senator]: "How could one not be here tonight when the occasion is to

Mathias and his hero, Abraham Lincoln (Johns Hopkins University Special Collections).

honor a great man, a man to whom so many ambassadors in Washington have turned to get wisdom and good advice—a man who could judge events from both a lofty point of view and with a great deal of common sense."
—*Emmanuel de Margerie, Ambassador of France*

[Citing Senator Mathias' election as president of the North Atlantic Assembly]: "How is it that this splendid American should be so much in demand on both sides of the Atlantic? [It is because] Mac makes of the Atlantic an ocean that does not divide us but binds us."
—*Sir Oliver Wright, Ambassador of Great Britain*

"Mac understands a great many things; Mac does his homework. He understood a long time ago a great deal about the nature of thermonuclear weapons. He understands the terminal quality of these weapons. He understands the great difficulty of getting along with the difficult Russian people, and he understands the complete necessity of coping with both of those great problems."
—*Thomas J. Watson, former head of IBM*

"We will miss him sorely in the Senate … but I must confess that I look forward to the day next January when I can address Mac as 'Professor Mathias' when our faculty and students at SAIS will have his wisdom and vision."
—*Steven J. Muller, President of Johns Hopkins University*

The following comments were among dozens entered into the Congressional Record in subsequent months by senators who were not able to attend the July dinner.

"Throughout his brilliant career, he has been a tireless and eloquent advocate of the rights of minorities, women, the elderly and the disabled. He has also been in the forefront on the continuing battle for equal voting rights for all citizens. Mac worked tirelessly to assure that Martin Luther King, Jr. received the recognition that he so richly deserved."
—*Senator Ted Kennedy (D-MA)*

"We respect the senior senator from Maryland for his well-known intellect. We respect him for his skill as a legislator. And we admire him for his prudence, wisdom, rock-steady temperament and ever-present good humor. But even more, Mac Mathias has made his mark as a man of conscience."
—*Senator Daniel Patrick Moynihan (D-NY)*

Additional Comment

"A cautious, wait-and-see attitude is characteristic of Senator Mathias, whose comments often lack precision until he is ready to take a stand."
—*Robert Timberg, article on Mathias and Reagan,*
Baltimore Evening Sun, *1980*

About the Contributors

Richard L. **Berke** is the co-founder and executive editor of STAT, a leading global news site that covers health and science. He got his start as a Washington correspondent for *The Baltimore Evening Sun*. He then spent 28 years at *The New York Times*, where he started as chief political correspondent. Later, he became an assistant managing editor for news, for features, Washington editor, national editor, and political editor. He was also executive editor of *Politico*.

Randolph Marshall **Collins** is the chief judge for the Pueblo of Acoma Tribal Court in New Mexico and teaches philosophy at New Mexico State University. Previously, he served as a trial prosecutor in New Mexico and as a civil litigation attorney in Washington, D.C. He held senior policy positions for Senator Mathias on the Senate Judiciary Committee staff and for Maryland Governor Schaefer.

Monica **Healy** was a senior legislative assistant for Senator Mathias for twelve years, later staff director of the Senate Democratic Policy Committee. She also held senior positions in the Clinton Administration, was director of the D.C. office for Maryland Gov. William Donald Schaefer and Vice President of Government Affairs for Teach For America.

Frederic B. **Hill** was a reporter, foreign correspondent and editorial writer for *The Baltimore Sun*. He then served as foreign affairs director for Senator Mathias in 1985 and 1986. He led an office in the Department of State that conducted wargaming exercises on national security issues from 1986 to 2006. He is the author of several books on Maine shipbuilding, shipwrecks, journalism and politics, including *The Life of Kings* and *Dereliction of Duty: The Failed Presidency of Donald John Trump*.

John **Hough**, Jr., was a staff writer for Senator Mathias from 1976 to 1977 and an assistant to James Reston at the Washington bureau of *The New York Times*. He is the author of seven novels, including *Seen the Glory: A Novel of the Battle of Gettysburg* and *The Sweetest Days*. He teaches creative writing.

Rep. Steny **Hoyer**, the highest-ranking and longest-serving U.S.

representative from Maryland in history, has represented the state's Fifth District since 1981. He has been the House majority leader, the House Democratic whip and chair of the House Democratic Caucus. Mr. Hoyer has been a staunch defender of civil rights, voting rights, and human rights, and an advocate of those with disabilities, and for protecting the Chesapeake Bay.

Stuart S. **Janney**, III, was a legislative assistant for Senator Mathias in 1973 and 1974. He then served as special assistant to Secretary of State Henry Kissinger. In 1977 and 1978 he was a legislative assistant for Senator Howard Baker. He practiced law and then joined Alex Brown & Sons, as head of asset management and managing director. He is chairman of Bessemer Trust.

Judith Davison **Keenan** worked for Senator Paul Sarbanes as a senior policy advisor and then became the executive director of the Joint Economic Committee. She has also worked on the Senate Banking Committee. She taught at colleges in the Democratic Republic of Congo and Niger.

Michael R. **Klipper** served as Senate Judiciary Committee counsel to Senator Mathias, from 1975 to 1982. The highlight of his Capitol Hill career was his work with Senator Mathias on the Voting Rights Amendments Act of 1982. Mr. Klipper served as in-house counsel to two leading trade associations, and he also engaged in the private law practice at a firm he co-founded. Throughout his career Mr. Klipper has been involved in myriad legal issues pertaining to copyright and constitutional law.

Steven J. **Metalitz** joined the Mathias staff in 1982 as counsel to the Criminal Law Subcommittee of the Senate Judiciary Committee. He was Senator Mathias' legislative director and chief counsel and staff director of Judiciary's Subcommittee on Patents, Copyrights and Trademarks. Following Mathias' retirement, Mr. Metalitz continued as Judiciary's Chief Nominations Counsel under chairman Joe Biden. He then became General Counsel of the Information Industry Association, and later entered private law practice.

Sen. Barbara **Mikulski** rose from her early career as a social worker in Baltimore in the 1960s to become the longest-serving woman in Congress, first as a member of the U.S. House, retiring in 2016 after five terms in the Senate. She worked to pass legislation to protect the most vulnerable members of society and to advance scientific research and democracy around the world. She was awarded the Presidential Medal of Freedom by President Obama in 2015. She is currently with Johns Hopkins University and was a Homewood Professor of Public Policy there.

Ann Terry **Pincus** was a journalist for many years, ranging from *The Arkansas Gazette* in Little Rock to *Glamour* magazine and Ridder Newspapers, covering congressional affairs in Washington. Later she wrote a column for *Working Woman* magazine and *The Village Voice*. She served as press secretary for Senator Mathias from 1983 to 1987. She was also a political appointee in the Clinton administration.

Sen. Alan K. **Simpson** served three terms (1979–1997) as a U.S. senator from Wyoming under four presidents—Carter, Reagan, (George H.W.) Bush and Clinton. He was assistant majority leader from 1984 to 1994. He chaired several committees and was the co-author of the first immigration reform legislation in 30 years. Upon his retirement, he was the director of the Institute for Policy Studies at Harvard's Kennedy School of Government.

Sen. Chris **Van Hollen** was elected to the U.S. Senate in November 2016 and reelected in 2022. He has authored significant legislation to combat climate change, protect the Chesapeake Bay, expand educational opportunities and advance equity in health care. He was in the U.S. House of Representatives prior to the Senate. Throughout his career, he has fought for social and racial justice, immigration reform, gun safety, human rights and campaign finance reform. He was a legislative aide to Senator Mathias on foreign policy and worked for Maryland Governor William Donald Schaefer.

Casimir **Yost** is an adjunct professor in the School of Foreign Service at Georgetown University. He directed the Institute for the Study of Diplomacy at Georgetown from 1994 to 2008 and now is a senior fellow. He was the director of the Strategic Futures Group of the National Intelligence Council in the Obama Administration. He served on the staff of Senator Mathias first in the personal office and then on the Senate Committee on Foreign Relations for a combined nine years.

Index